ANIMAL GRACE

Also by Mary Lou Randour

Women's Psyche, Women's Spirit:
The Reality of Relationships

Exploring Sacred Landscapes:
Religious and Spiritual Experiences in Psychotherapy

ANIMAL GRACE

Entering a Spiritual Relationship
with Our Fellow Creatures

MARY LOU RANDOUR

Foreword by SUSAN CHERNAK McELROY

NEW WORLD LIBRARY
NOVATO, CALIFORNIA

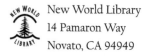 New World Library
14 Pamaron Way
Novato, CA 94949

Library of Congress Cataloging-in-Publication Data
Randour, Mary Lou.
 Animal grace : entering a spiritual relationship with our fellow creatures / Mary Lou Randour ; foreword by Susan Chernak McElroy.
 p. cm.
 Includes bibliographic references and index.
 ISBN 1-57731-104-3 (perfect : alk. paper)
 1. Animals — Religious aspects. 2. Human-animal relationships — Religious aspects. I. Title.
BL439.R36 1999
291.2'12—dc21   99-049172
                                                                                    CIP

First printing, February 2000
ISBN 1-57731-104-3
Printed in the U.S.A. on acid-free paper
Distributed to the trade by Publishers Group West

10 9 8 7 6 5 4 3 2 1

For the animals

Contents

Foreword

This fall morning in Wyoming is cold. Low clouds touch the tips of the quaking aspens and a heavy, glass-like dew bends the yellowed grasses in our pastures. I pull on a thick sweatshirt and a canvas hat, call the dogs, and head out for the chicken shed. When I pull open the henhouse door, a dozen hearty banty hens spill out, pecking eagerly at the earwigs holed up in the rickety doorframe. The colors of the small hens are brilliant: gold and black, white with coffee-brown speckles, mottled grays and silvers, and — my personal favorite — a tiny Rhode Island Red the color of polished mahogany. In the moments I take to watch their morning rituals of stretching, preening, and dust bathing, I feel my breathing deepen. The hens' focus, and their utter attention to this moment, becomes mine as well.

Up at the barn, the donkeys are honking. The sound is like a truck engine that won't quite crank over. Polani, my tiny gray donkey, always ends her braying with a plaintive, choking sob. Her sister Aurora brays like wind moaning through sailboat rigging. When the dogs and I get to the barn, the sobbing and moaning is in full chorus. Good God, you'd think I only fed them once a year.

The pastures are still productive, but everyone wants hay. I'm happy to oblige. I love the sound of animals eating hay. It is a sound that says, at least within the confines of this small barn, that all is right with the world. By the time the hay is in the mangers, my old mare has shuffled into the corral. I pull down a bucket full of grooming tools and go to work on her, focusing completely on the richness of her brown coat, the smoothness of her muscles, the feel of her coarse, black tail and mane. She is eighteen years old and creaky with arthritis. One bum knee has taken some of the grace out of her stride, yet I can easily imagine her as the racetrack princess she once was. Back then, an up-and-coming superstar, she was pampered and treated like royalty. Now, her pampering is in my hands and fussing over her is my joy. Not because she runs like the wind. She doesn't. But she once ran like the wind and has now put all that behind her to live her elder years — her years of most inspiring dignity — with me. To spend time with an old animal is to know wisdom firsthand. I treasure my mornings with this mare, delighting in the comfort and security I can bring to her last, full years.

Yesterday when I entered the barn, it was filled with magpies. I love these birds that remind me so much of flying orcas, with their splendid black-and-white plumage. One young bird was perched on Polani's behind. Two more cackled in the loft. Three sat atop a huge nest of twigs and small branches woven into the barn rafters, where all six had hatched last spring. I remember locking the barn cat in our house as those babies grew, determined that Sammi would not get his claws into them. When the young birds left their nest one by one and plopped onto the barn floor, I gently carried them to a small stand of aspens where they would be safe from the foxes and weasels that hunt around our corrals. Twice, their ferocious magpie mother bloodied my head as I carried her babies to safety. Now, the whole family had returned home, bolder than I ever imagined them to be. Not one budged as I passed beneath them and grabbed three flakes of hay, stuffed the mangers, and then began flinging manure into the garden cart. Instead, they watched me intently, muttering what sounded like almost-human whispers. To see them in all their robust, juvenile glory was an unexpected blessing. I chose to imagine they had come back to say hello and to let me know that all of them were doing just fine, thank you.

I used to look at my farm chores as pleasant interludes in a too-busy life, as moments for enchantment and introspection. After reading *Animal Grace* by Mary Lou Randour, I find that I have yet another way to define these precious moments: Barn chores are an important part of my spiritual practice.

Randour believes, as I do, that we do not work on our spiritual lives in isolation. Spirituality is a relationship with self, Creator, and others. Much of my spiritual practice — the part of my practice that involves compassion and service — centers on my relationship with "others" — with animals. It looks like chores, or tending to adventurous baby birds, or shoveling manure, but it is spiritual practice. I try to undertake each task with the "other" in mind. To see my animal companions living in health and joy is a source of deep fulfillment for me. Each stall cleaned, each water bowl filled, each meal prepared with no meat is a compassionate service I perform mindfully for my animal family. These animal companions are precious, living pieces of the larger face of God before me, and I am honored to be in service to them.

Animal Grace beautifully charts Randour's illuminating journey along her spiritual path of animal grace. In its pages, I found many ghosts of my own spiritual odyssey along what I call the "four-footed path." Although focused on animals, Randour's story is one I will eagerly share with any friend searching for a spiritual homecoming. Service, compassion, and awareness, no matter where or to whom we render them, are the cornerstones of a soul-filled existence.

Like many others, I have fretted that I seem to have so little time to devote to my spiritual pursuits. My spiritual practices have included reading, meditating, reflection, group meetings of like-minded souls, retreats, and a list of other pastimes that all seem to take me out of my daily routine. Randour reminds us that the common fabric of daily life can be filled with spiritual awakenings of small and large proportions. We can choose to see our many activities as sacred acts, imbued with spiritual teachings and lessons. Our actions are our daily conversation with the divine, and in the instant we choose to recognize this, the simplest acts of the most ordinary day become prayers. In this fashion, my barn duties are no longer chores. They are my gifts to my animal companions and my conversations with God.

Animal Grace, and the philosophy it explores, is a welcome and deeply needed counterpoint to our skewed cultural myths about our relationship with animals, spirit, and our environment. Although many religious traditions remind us that we are all one, I don't think many members of what we call "civilized" humankind have a deeply felt sense of what this great truth means. Living as we do in a computerized, mechanized, competition-driven culture, we fall easily into the absurd idea that the rest of the world — the world of spirit, soul, and nature — is as competitive and judgment-oriented as we are. Books like *Animal Grace* have the magic to dispel that dangerous myth. They return us to that quiet place in our hearts where we recognize animals and the rest of living creation as our brothers and sisters.

It is this felt sense, and only this felt sense, that can return us to holy ground in our minds, hearts, and lives. Knowledge and education are fine as far as they go, but only feeling — an emotional understanding — will lead us to the land of new visions and to the shores of wisdom. *Animal Grace* is a thoughtful, beautiful guidebook to this sacred landscape.

— Susan Chernak McElroy
Author of *Animals As Teachers and Healers*
Brightstar Farm, Wyoming

Acknowledgments

Writing a book is a group effort, even though there may be only one author listed. This certainly was the case with *Animal Grace.* I am grateful to Sam Black, my life partner, who shares my commitment to animals. His unwavering faith in me kept me going. He also responded to my repeated requests for help in thinking through various topics, and read and commented on various stages of my manuscript, with a generosity of spirit I could only hope to emulate.

I also am indebted to my sister and best friend, Carole Dickson, also an animal lover and protector. Her love and confidence fortified me. She also shared her home in Florida with me, where I spent much of the winter working on my book, and where we experimented with many new recipes, savoring the results together. Her comments about my writing also helped shape my thinking.

Many other friends deserve my thanks. J. R. Hyland commented on drafts and set me straight on proper biblical references and terms; Mary E. Hunt's friendship and advice sustained me; Carol Adams, who became a friend in the process of writing this book, also encouraged me; Martha Young, who started out as my valued copy editor, became a friend as well; and Roxanne Farmanfarmaian generously took time for me and offered suggestions for prospective publishers.

Toshi and Sophie, my canine companions, were often my inspiration and frequently reminded me, as only 100-pound dogs can, that it was time to stop writing about a relationship with animals and start enjoying one.

I can't imagine having a more satisfying, and easier, relationship with an editor than I did with Jason Gardner. He gave me feedback with such great skill and diplomacy that I always awaited his comments with eager anticipation. His editing not only made my writing more graceful and precise, his suggestion to me to "show" not "tell" greatly improved the tone, making my message more effective. I also am grateful to Katharine Farnam Conolly for her contribution, and to the staff of New World Library for their enthusiasm for this project.

Although my parents, Arthur and Pearle, died many years ago, I see their influence on me, perhaps now more than ever. I am thankful to them for many things, but probably most of all for teaching me by their example about the importance of fair play and common decency.

Introduction

Until very recently I never quite understood what "grace" meant, though I certainly heard it often used in the Episcopal church in which I was raised. Even as a child, I picked up the weighty significance of the word "grace" from the tone of the voices uttering it. As I grew older, I couldn't help but notice that many people used grace to explain a monumental spiritual event in someone's life. Grace seemed to be the key — perhaps not the only one, but certainly one of the most important — to entering a spiritual life. It was a key, however, I could not find.

My failure to find the meaning of grace was just the tip of a spiritual iceberg, a term I use deliberately. Although I searched for a spiritual home, my heart was frozen. No spiritual message, religious image, or theological understanding could penetrate me. My mind remained open as I sought out various points of view from many different traditions — process theology and feminist theology in Christianity, the Jewish mysticism of Martin Buber, and both the theory and practice of Buddhism. But these teachings never found their way to the place within me where I really lived, my vital center. I continued to perceive an impenetrable object between the essential "I" and a *felt* sense of spirituality, despite my best efforts to keep an open mind, and despite my longing for a spiritual insight that would resonate deeply in my being.

What we know we know through our bodies, according to psychologist Ken Shapiro, who draws upon the field of phenomenology. It is in and through our bodies that we first organize meaning, before we transform our experience into language.[1] Meaning does not originate in the head; rather, it travels from the body to the head, through the heart. And I simply could not open my heart.

Eventually I grew resigned, giving up hope that I would ever experience the felt sense of spirituality I craved. Instead I learned to live with the feeling of reaching for something that seemed always beyond my grasp. As I lived with this loss, I continued to read occasionally about spirituality, and to wonder. These readings taught me that spiritual awakenings often come unexpectedly and apparently without our conscious effort. And so it was with me.

Although there are really no precise beginnings in these matters, my story began a number of years ago, when I started donating to animal advocacy groups, one of the types of charities to which I contributed. When their literature came in the mail, I would scan it, noticing the endless stream of suffering to which animals seemed to be subjected — but I didn't really absorb it. I continued contributing, and eventually other animal advocacy groups began sending me their literature. More envelopes with heart-stopping, stomach-wrenching images crossed my desk: starving, beaten dogs ready to collapse; a cat, her head bolted to a metal frame, a wired device implanted in the top of her skull, her eyes open, startled, and unblinking; rabbits with ugly, red ulcerations eating away at their bodies in order to test cosmetics or household products.

Mail saturated with these images kept coming and, in time, I began to pause longer before the graphic pictures of animal suffering, unable to turn away quite as quickly as I had before. The more I lingered, the more distressed I became. Finally these accumulating images impelled me to read a book I had always meant to read, *Animal Liberation* by Peter Singer.[2] I expected reading *Animal Liberation*, a moral philosophy for animal rights, would be an intellectual endeavor. It was, but its considerable intellectual power paled in comparison to the emotional and spiritual effect it had on me; it was an effect I had not anticipated. Intuitively, I had picked up this book at a moment when I was prepared to hear its message.

Spiritual awakenings don't happen in isolation; rather, they appear in the context of relationships. When we are ready, the relationship generates a spiritual event.[3] Through *Animal Liberation*, I formed a relationship with all of the animals whose lives intersected with mine. As my awareness developed, the animals taught me that my decisions affected them.

The protective membrane of statistics that shielded me from the agony of the animals and allowed me to maintain my otherness had been ripped away. These statistics were no longer just startling numbers; behind the numbers were suffering animals. Now, with nothing between them and me, I felt a dramatic and unfamiliar shift in awareness and intensity. I was with them, in the midst of their agony, fear, helplessness, and bewilderment. In the beginning of this journey, I often wept inconsolably as I tried to fall asleep. Instead of experiencing restful slumber, I plummeted into the tortured world of needless animal suffering that had been opened to me. Now I knew — all too well — how intimately involved we humans are with animals, that we use them to test makeup and floor cleaners, to conduct medical and psychological research, to "perform" in circuses, to supply us with food and fur. The sheer number of animals we use up is staggering: twenty-five million a year in medical research and product and cosmetic testing; seven billion slaughtered for food annually; thousands seized from their natural habitat and confined in circuses and zoos.[4]

A spiritual opportunity lay at the center of this world of animal suffering. Speaking to me through their suffering, the animals opened my heart and gave me the chance to overcome my spiritual impasse. Despite its undeniable emotional difficulty, I realized that my new-found awareness was, quite simply, a spiritual gift. Zen monk and peace activist Thich Nhat Hanh has observed that one cannot grow, or achieve peace, without suffering, saying: "We may need to transform suffering into insight, insight into nonduality, insight that leads to compassion."[5]

I learned that as we gain access to our hearts and minds, by acknowledging the ways in which we affect the lives of animals, this knowledge benefits us as much as it does the animals. As a psychologist, I know that a divided self cannot operate at its fullest potential. When we divide ourselves by denying, avoiding, repressing, or disassociating, we weaken our psychological capacity. It takes psychic energy to not know, or to not care, or to not act. When we allow ourselves to know, care, and act, we release energy, making it available for the growth and nurturance of our psychological and spiritual selves.

I returned to my spiritual search with strengthened conviction; my heart, no longer frozen, beat purposefully. I committed myself to relieving the unnecessary suffering of the animals, knowing that I must build my own internal resources to help them. I learned first hand what Andrew Linzey, a preeminent animal theologian, had said: Once you take the road of becoming aware, *really* aware, of animal suffering, it is a one-way street. There is no turning back. There is, however, a moving forward toward a more committed and better articulated spirituality.

One day I noticed within myself a quiet tranquillity. As I accomplished the different activities of my day — my practice of psychology, personal chores, and animal advocacy — I felt serene, strong, and in possession of a seemingly limitless still energy. Turning to my husband as we were walking the dogs together, I said: "Now, at long last I think I know what grace is. How I feel right now is grace. This is it. And I know it won't last. But now I know it's possible." Although this moment of grace came to me without effort or will, I know that it grew out of a process — at once subtle and distinct. Although I believe this process is life-long, I also am convinced that a turning point occurred when I committed myself to helping relieve the suffering of animals. My work on behalf of animals infused me with a sense of purpose and prepared me to accept my own spiritual energy.

Joanna Macy, known for her work on Buddhism and ecology, has described this sensation of grace as finding "oneself empowered to act on behalf of other beings — or on behalf of the larger whole — and the empowerment itself seems to come 'through' that or those for whose sake one acts."[6] Through their suffering, the animals I had come to see and hear had given me the gift of grace and resurrected my spiritual search. They gave to me. I would do what I could to give to them in return.

Animals have much to teach us. They also possess the capacity to heal us. We know that animals play an important role in teaching children empathy. They can also enhance self-esteem and aid those who undergo coronary surgery in their recovery. Their presence can touch our souls, heal our psyches, and restore our bodies. In my case, the animals I encountered reconnected me to something fundamental within myself — that innermost aspect of my being that yearned for wholeness, a wholeness that only can be achieved through spiritual work. Animals are, as author Susan Chernak McElroy has observed, "embodiments of grace and blessing."[7]

Even when we cannot yet perceive that which begs to be acknowledged, I sense that all of us persist in "yearning for wholeness," desiring to be more connected to all of creation.[8] I now know, from my own felt experience, that grace-filled spiritual possibilities appear when we redirect our attention toward the effect our actions have on the lives of animals. In so doing, we recapture the relationship we have with *all* of life, not just human life. This is a mutual process: As we become more aware of and responsible to the animals that surround our lives, they in turn teach us and heal us by redirecting us to the vitality of creation.

Our spiritual relationship with animals builds on two basic commitments: to expand awareness and to take compassionate action. Awareness without any response can become isolating and self-indulgent. The pejorative phrase "navel-gazing" captures this concern. Someone might spend hours sitting on a cushion or praying in church to achieve a clear mind, but once achieved, stop there. A clear mind is not the end of one's spiritual story but its beginning.

At the same time, individuals who take action without the benefit of awareness or clarity put themselves, as well as their mission, in peril. Without awareness one can too easily fall into dogmatic positions that harden the opposition and betray the very purpose of taking action, which is to cultivate greater justice and compassion in this world. Taking action also often means confronting opposition or indifference, which can be difficult and depleting. All who take action will need to replenish themselves.

Those interested in pursuing spirituality through one's relationship with animals don't have to do anything special. A spiritual relationship with animals is foremost a practice rooted in the everyday — we can act spiritually as we engage in the daily, mundane activities of our lives. It is in these ordinary events that we find extraordinary spiritual possibilities. Our expanding awareness will allow us, for example, to choose to buy products not tested on animals. We also can decide to eat different food. We can firmly say "No!" to suffering. In these and other ways, we can take compassionate action. With each act, we deepen our awareness, strengthen our compassion, and enrich our spirituality. By making a spiritual relationship with animals an integral part of our practice, we find the opportunity, and encouragement, to recognize and revere the sacredness of all life.

Of course all of creation has intrinsic value and deserves our attention. We should open ourselves to animals for two reasons, either one of which is sufficient in itself. First, so many animals have undergone such unrecognized suffering. As John Cobb, an eminent Christian theologian, has pleaded: "Hundreds of millions of suffering animals cry out to the Christian community to pay attention and to care."[9]

Jewish and Buddhist writers have made the same appeal to their faith communities. Isaac Bashevis Singer, winner of the Nobel Prize for literature, saw an inescapable link between the treatment of animals and human moral development: "As long as human beings will go on shedding the blood of animals, there will never be any peace. There is only one little step from killing animals to creating gas chambers à la Hitler and concentration camps à la Stalin.... There will be no justice as long as man will stand with a knife or gun and destroy those who are weaker than he is."[10] Roshi Philip Kapleau, Buddhist monk, teacher, and writer, also makes a case for the end to the slaughter and eating of animals. In his book *To Cherish All Life*, he reminds us that the first precept of Buddhism is not to kill, or harm, any living being. It is "a call to life and creation even as it is a condemnation of death and destruction."[11]

Second, animals have a wisdom that is, as yet, largely undiscovered by some, and unexplored by others. In many ways their sensory world is vastly different from ours. In that difference, animals have access to levels of reality that might remain hidden to us without their help. I know this from my own experience with my dog, Toshi. Many years ago my husband and I had a dear friend, Robin, who was dying of cancer. We knew her death was imminent. One quiet night I lay reading in bed, as Toshi slept on his dog bed nearby. Suddenly, he awoke, sat up, threw back his head, and began a plaintive howling. Initially startled, I watched him to see if he was okay. After a number of mournful cries, Toshi settled back into his bed, and returned to sleep. The next morning we got a call from Robin's partner, who told us that she had died the previous evening at about 10:30. Toshi's howling took place at 10:45. He knew something I did not and he was able to point me toward a new understanding — that there is no exact moment of death in which we no longer exist. Rather, death is a transition to another state and that if we are sensitive enough we can participate in that transition. It is a lesson that I continue to ponder and attempt to understand.

In *Animal Grace*, I hope to build upon the groundwork that so many before me have provided.[12] I am indebted to them for many reasons. The obvious one is that their work provided a vast amount of thought and information that I have used in writing this book. Less obviously, but more fundamentally, they exposed me to ideas that reawakened me spiritually, and I am deeply grateful to them for their part in my spiritual journey. This journey is a process about which I feel deeply, care passionately, and think as mindfully as I can. While it is not always easy, it is always fulfilling. Our spiritual relationship with animals presents yet one more opportunity to commit oneself to life; it is one that is too good to pass up.[13]

I hope that in the following chapters of *Animal Grace* you will derive some inspiration for making this journey of the spirit. Chapter 1, "What Animals Can Teach Us about Spirituality," details the many wondrous ways in which animals have demonstrated that they are our spiritual teachers and healers. Their message to us is this: If you let us, we can teach you how to love, reunite you with nature, impart essential lessons about death and dying, contribute to your physical health and psychological well-being, and help you grow up. Building on this first chapter, chapter 2, "Entering a Spiritual Relationship with Animals," lays out a structure for becoming spiritually engaged with our fellow creatures. This structure is built on two pillars: developing awareness and taking compassionate action. I propose that through our spiritual relationship with animals we can heighten our sensibilities to the seamless wonder of creation and our part in it.

The next three chapters, "The Peaceable *Kindom*," "The New Kashrut," and "*Ahimsa*," revolve around three religious concepts. "The Peaceable *Kindom*" discusses the vision, as articulated by Isaiah, of a time when all creation will live together in harmony, without violence or conflict. Modern-day versions of peaceable kingdoms are presented, along with how to evoke the peaceable kingdom in our lives.

Many paths may lead us toward the goal of a more peaceable kindom. One of these is the system of *kashrut*, as articulated in the Jewish tradition, which reminds us that the act of eating should be hallowed and that the production, preparation, and consumption of food are spiritual acts. Chapter 4 describes the origins of this principle in the Hebrew Bible and texts and shows how the spirit of kashrut also appears in other major religious systems of thought. Finally, I detail the spiritual benefits that can be gained from practicing a new kashrut of vegetarianism, one that is based on a reverence for life, a respect for the environment, and a desire for social justice.

Perhaps the bedrock principle underlying all major religious tenets, and the basis for a spiritual relationship with animals, is that of *ahimsa* — the practice of refraining from harming other living beings, or from taking another being's life. Chapter 5 documents the origins of this great moral principle of nonviolence as well as its integral elements — the recognition of the continuity of existence, the link to karma, and the requirement to love your enemy. Examples of ahimsa are offered throughout the chapter as well as ways in which to put ahimsa into practice in one's daily life.

A book on developing a spiritual relationship with animals would not be complete without discussing the spiritual lives and soulful natures of our animal kin. "The Souls and Spiritual Lives of Animals" explores the role of "spirit" animals throughout human history. It also discusses support for the idea that animals possess spiritual attributes, drawing upon various schools of Hinduism, Buddhism, and the Judeo-Christian tradition.

In order to place our discussion in the context of everyday living, and as a way to demonstrate the very practical nature of this spiritual proposal, *Animal Grace* concludes with chapter 7, "The Parallel Worlds of Human and Nonhuman Animals," introducing the character Eve. We follow Eve through a typical day, seeing how the mundane decisions she makes about what kind of food to eat, clothes to buy, or products to use, affect a variety of animals existing in a world parallel to hers. Eve could be any one of us; she is a spiritual seeker and well-intended person, yet at the beginning of the chapter at times

Chapter One

What Animals Can Teach Us about Spirituality

Animals have been the spiritual companions of humans since the beginning of recorded time. The earliest indication of the spiritual significance of the human-animal relationship can be found in the 20,000-year-old cave wall paintings of Cro-Magnon people. In many if not most cultures, animals have served a variety of spiritual functions: They have been linked with supernatural forces, acted as guardians and shamans, and appeared in images of an afterlife. They have even been worshipped as agents of gods and goddesses.[1] Many ancient creation myths, for example, depict God with a dog. These stories do not explain the existence of the dog; like God, the dog is assumed to have existed from the beginning. In this assumption, these primordial people revealed their intense attachment to their animal companions.[2]

That animals touch us in a deep, central place is not a modern-day phenomenon, but one that pervades the history of the human-animal relationship. We sense that we can benefit spiritually in our relationship with animals, and we are right. They offer us something fundamental: a direct and immediate sense of both the joy and wonder of creation. We recognize that animals seem to feel more intensely and purely than we do. Perhaps we yearn to express ourselves with such abandon and integrity. Animals fully reveal to us what we already glimpse: it is feeling — and the organization of feeling — that forms the core of self. We also sense that through our relationship to animals we can recover that which is true within us and, through the discovery of that truth, find our spiritual direction. Quite simply, animals teach us about love: how to love, how to enjoy being loved, how loving itself is an activity that generates more love, radiating out and encompassing an ever larger circle of others. Animals propel us into an "economy of abundance."[3]

They teach us the language of the spirit. Through our contact with animals we can learn to overcome the limits imposed by difference; we can reach beyond the walls we have erected between the mundane and the sacred. They can even help us stretch ourselves to discover new frontiers of consciousness. Animals cannot "talk" to us, but they can communicate with us and commune with us in a language that does not require words. They help us understand that words might even stand in the way.

Lois Crisler did not use human words to achieve a spiritual connection with animals. Instead, she used their language. Sitting in a tent with her husband one twilight morning in Alaska, she heard a sound she had never heard before — the howl of a wolf. Thrilled, she stepped outside the tent and impulsively howled in return, "pouring out my wilderness loneliness." She was answered by a chorus of wolves' voices, yodeling in a range of low, medium, and high notes. Other wolves joined in, each at a different pitch. "The wild deep medley of chords," she recalls, "…the absence of treble, made a strange, savage, heart-stirring uproar."[4] It was the "roar of nature," a roar that brings us back to an essential place we have known but lost. It returns us to nature and to creation, not intellectually but viscerally. We recollect in the cells of our bodies, not in our heads. If we open to it, we can make out the image of our animal kin by our side.

Fulfilling our longing for the wild, our primordial desire to hear "the roar of nature" within ourselves, does not require that we camp out in Alaska, or even encounter an animal in its natural habitat. Spiritual contact with an animal can happen under quite ordinary circumstances.

I once took a yoga class while visiting my sister in Sarasota, Florida, in a beautiful studio with floor-to-ceiling windows. As the class was engaged in exercise, we noticed a dog standing outside the window, innocently looking in. The dog seemed curious, and wagged his tail in a relaxed motion. Soon, he was joined by another dog, who also watched us through the window. Occasionally one or the other would bark — not a loud bark, but a "here I am" kind of bark. For the entire hour-and-a-half session they stood there, noses to the glass, looking in with interest. They seemed calm, but intensely attentive, and clearly interested in joining us. One could assign any number of explanations to their absorbed interest. I think, as did others in the class, that they picked up on some kind of "positive energy" generated by our collective yoga practice. I put quotes around "positive energy" because I don't have precise language to describe what I think the dogs sensed. And that is the point. They were able to perceive, and experience, something some of us are dimly aware of and would like to understand, but cannot find words to describe. Animals can teach us to live outside of words, to listen to other forms of consciousness, to tune into other rhythms.

It was the rhythm of music that one musician, Jim Nollman, used to communicate with whales. Along with several other musicians, he recorded hours of human-orca music in an underwater studio every summer for twelve years. Positioning their boat so that the whales would approach them, the group transmitted their music through the water. Most of the time the orcas made the same sounds, regardless of whether the music was played or not. But not all the time. For a few minutes every year, a "sparkling communication occurred. In one instance, the sound of an electric guitar note elicited responses from several whales. In another, an orca joined with the musicians, 'initiat[ing] a melody and rhythm over a blues progression, empha-sizing the chord changes.'"5

An uncanny meeting with a whale proved a decisive spiritual moment for another person, a retired female teacher who I have enjoyed hiking with in northern California. While hiking along the ocean, she decided to rest on a large, flat rock jutting out over the depths. She lay there, relaxed, listening to the sound of the water and the sensation of the breeze on her body when, she reports, she felt a presence: "The hairs on the back of my neck went up; I was compelled to sit up." Sitting up, she saw a whale, resting perpendicular on her fluke. As her eyes met the whale's, time stopped. As they gazed at each other, the woman entered an eternal stillness, feeling an unmatched intensity. Difference dissolved; words were irrelevant. She felt a deep sense of connection with all of life. No longer restricted by the categories of "them" and "us," she felt herself flow into a seamless web of existence in which all of life is one. In complete harmony with the whale, this retired teacher felt that she inhabited a web of relations some call "God." She had encountered God in, and through, the eyes of a whale.

Cross-species communication may be so extraordinary because we cannot rely on identifying with the creature the way we identify with human beings for connection. Our human relationships are often based on relating to a being like ourselves: We can identify and empathize with each other because we share similar experiences. Of course, there is nothing wrong with this. The ability to identify with others forms the basis for personal relationships, social bonds, and social justice.

Animals, however, offer us a unique opportunity to transcend the boundaries of our human perspectives; they allow us to stretch our consciousness toward understanding what it is like to be different. This stretching enables us to grow beyond our narrow viewpoint. It allows us, I believe, to gain a spiritual advantage. How can we possibly appreciate and move toward spiritual wholeness if we cannot see beyond our own species? How can we come to know God, or grasp the interconnectedness of all life, if we limit ourselves to knowing only our own kind? The goal of compassion is not to care because someone is like us but to care because they are themselves.

Any spiritual discipline, in any tradition, invites us to open our hearts and minds. This invitation represents an ongoing exercise; the desire and attempt to open to others in our midst are the essence of the spiritual process.

Animals can lead us spiritually in a variety of ways. As we will see, they can teach us about death, participate in our social and moral development, enhance our physical and psychological well-being, and heighten our capacity to love and to experience joy.

Death Lessons

I recounted earlier how my dog, Toshi, howled inexplicably, seemingly without external provocation, a few minutes after a friend died in a distant city. Stephen Levine, Buddhist practitioner and author, writes:

> Those who know the process directly — from experiences shared with the dying, from decades of meditation, from moments of spontaneous grace from eucharists of every description — do not speak of death as a single moment before which you are alive and after which you are not. They refer instead to a 'point of remembrance' in which the holding of life transforms into a letting go into death.[6]

This is what Toshi taught me: that death is not a single moment, but a process of transformation, from a holding on to a letting go into some new form. Of course, I still do not exactly understand the transformation. And I am not entirely comfortable with any one particular system of thought that attempts to explain this phenomenon. But Toshi's howling — which I understand as his ability to tune into our friend's spirit as it was making its transformation — encouraged me to keep an open mind as I continue to pursue my questions about the meaning of death. This experience with Toshi, and others that have followed and built upon it, has also helped me to decide that when a loved one of mine has died, with their prior permission, I will not abandon his or her body. Instead I will stay with the body, meditating, praying, touching it, participating in the transition that the person's consciousness (human or animal) is making. And I want the same for myself.

Another experience with a dog, much earlier in my life, at age sixteen, also taught me a lesson about death. This time the dog was not my companion but a stranger who turned up in my backyard in the middle of the night. A few weeks prior to this nighttime visit, my paternal grandfather had died, the first death of a human member of our family.

Like many teenagers, in adolescence I became obsessed with death and dying; I wondered and worried about it. Basically I just didn't like the idea, or any of the subsequent options I envisioned for myself: death as extinction, death as "bliss" in some cartoon-like heaven, or, alternatively, death as hell. Living forever, which I understood wasn't an option, also didn't seem very desirable. I was stuck.

Then, soon after my grandfather died, I awoke from a sound sleep in the middle of the night. I didn't know what had awakened me. I remember my room was filled with moonlight. I felt compelled to stand up and gaze out my window, which overlooked the backyard. My family lived in a row house, with a house on either side of us, and a fence dividing our backyards.

As I looked down I saw a collie, sitting, his face lifted toward my window. We stared at one another for one eternally long, still moment. I recall the intensity of that moment, and the brilliance of the moonlight. Although I looked down from the second floor, I felt as though the collie and I were separated only by inches. A thought flickered through my mind that perhaps I should be frightened. One part of my brain was observing this scene, noting its eerie quality. But the question of whether or not I should be afraid quickly dissolved into a realization: "There is no reason to be afraid; this is my grandfather." We sat for another long moment. Then the dog turned and jumped over the fence, clearing it by feet, not inches. But he never landed on the other side. As I watched, he seemed to evaporate into air.

I stood before the window, stunned. "I must be dreaming," I thought. Making a mental and physical check of myself, I confirmed that I wasn't. On reflection, my dead grandfather appearing to me in the form of a collie — fantastic in and of itself — was not as significant as the fact that I wasn't afraid. I, who was terrified and tortured by my thoughts of death, felt no apprehension. I felt calm and at peace. I returned to bed and fell asleep.

At first, I didn't speak to anyone about what happened, probably because it seemed too incredible to be believed. Eventually I told a few people. Each time I recounted the story, I didn't expect anyone to believe me. I almost don't believe me! Except that I was there, and when I recall that moment of inexplicable knowledge, which comes back so vividly, I have no doubts.

I can't say that the visit had any profound spiritual effect on me at the time. I don't think I was able to absorb the lesson that was offered to me. It has been only recently, with my experience of Toshi's howling and my continued spiritual seeking, that I have begun to assimilate this lesson. While a howling dog might not prove to be as decisive for others as it was for me, I think there are two reasons for my conclusion. First, I believe I was simply ready to find a lesson in Toshi's howling after our friend's death. I had been thinking about death, and what it means, since adolescence. After all those years of sorting through my thoughts and feelings, I was prepared to learn something from this experience. The other reason is that Toshi, more than any other dog I have known, possesses some quality — an intuition and sensitivity — that I find spiritual.

This is what I think it means for me: I may never know during this life the exact nature of the transformation of death, whether it is a type of reincarnation, or one's consciousness entering a vast stream of consciousness. Whatever it is, we don't have to be afraid of death. The body dies, and the spirit, or consciousness, transforms.

I also don't know why the lesson came to me in the form of a dog. What I do understand is that I received the most meaningful lesson possible: not to fear death. My job will be to wrestle with that lesson for the rest of my life — continually turning my mind over, opening myself to experience, reading all I can. I do all of this with gratitude for the extraordinary gift given to me by my dog teachers.

Lessons about dying are really lessons about living — living fully, openly, gratefully. This is the lesson that author Susan Chernak McElroy learned from Keesha, a German shepherd, who was her "confidant…angel and…teacher." Diagnosed in 1988 with a usually fatal neck cancer, McElroy was initially at a loss. Her doctors didn't expect her to survive two years. No one among her family or friends had ever faced a life-threatening illness. "Where," she wondered, "was I to find examples of how to live what was left of my life?" She turned to her memory of Keesha, who had died years earlier of cancer.

One of Keesha's pleasures as a healthy dog was swimming in the deep lagoons near her home. At the end of her illness, Keesha was severely debilitated and too frail to enjoy such play. But that didn't mean that Keesha was too frail to find joy in what she *could* do. Instead of the lagoon, Keesha found pleasure jumping in the puddles of water that filled the streets near their home. With a look of pure bliss, Keesha would frolic in the water, barking in joy, for as long as she was allowed. "From a dog splashing in a rain puddle," McElroy recounts, "I learned about choice. Regardless of how much time I had left, I could choose to celebrate whatever possibilities life had to offer me each moment….The antidote to fear is to practice joy in the moment." Following Keesha's example, McElroy not only survived her cancer, she learned how to live — with less apprehension and with more wonder and joy.[7]

Healing and Well-Being

I've seen the picture: a somewhat gangly teenage boy with close-cropped hair and an impassive face clumsily holding a small black-and-white mutt. The dog, who is part of a pet-facilitated therapy program, has just been introduced to this fifteen-year-old boy. The hope is that by learning to comfortably touch, care for, and love this animal the boy can learn to love himself and others. The boy needs help badly; he is in this program because he has murdered someone.

I also have seen a different picture of the same boy and the same dog, taken a few months after the initial meeting. This time the boy tenderly holds the dog, his arms wrapped around her, his face buried in her shoulder. The boy seeks comfort and the dog quietly provides it. The author Jeffrey Masson, who has written *Dogs Never Lie About Love*, claims that "the dog *is* love, that dogs are all about love."[8] The dog, through her generous capacity to love freely, completely, trustingly, is teaching the boy to love. The dog is healing his soul.

Increasingly, we humans are sharing our lives with dogs. Currently 52 million dogs reside in American households. Simply through their central role in our lives, dogs play a central role in our healing and well-being. But it isn't just dogs who can heal us: horses and dolphins, to name a few other species, also have that capacity.

Meredith, a five-year-old girl, underwent multiple surgeries to correct a congenital facial deformity. Not only were the surgeries a terrible ordeal, but Meredith also felt ashamed of her condition. Her mother found the help she sought for her daughter in a horse. In learning to ride and care for the horse, Meredith blossomed. She became self-confident, stronger, and better able to face her condition. The horse's calm, accepting presence gave Meredith something she could not find elsewhere.[9]

That animals can literally heal us and bolster our well-being is not the stuff of fiction, or the occasional news report. Scientists are carefully gathering growing evidence of the psychological and physiological benefits of our relationship with animals.

One scientist studying animals' effect on human health, psychologist Karen Allen, has discovered a variety of benefits provided by companion animals. In one study, Allen examined the effect of animals on the blood pressure of elderly people. We know that blood pressure increases as a result of aging, and that these increases can be reduced through strong social support. Allen found that elderly people with pet dogs and cats but no human social contact nevertheless enjoyed the same reduced blood pressure.[10]

Of course, you don't have to wait until you are elderly to receive benefits from animal companionship. Allen found that middle-aged women and married couples also gained from their relationship with animals. One group of women were asked to perform a mental arithmetic test while scientists measured their heart rate, skin conductance, and blood pressure, all indicators of stress or relaxation. Scientists had the women perform the test by themselves, then in the presence of a friend, and then with their companion dog at their side. By now you have probably guessed that the women were most relaxed in the presence of their pets — even more relaxed than with their friends.[11] A similar study with married couples found that, once again, canine friends proved to be better at helping someone relax than spouses. In fact, wives and husbands had the lowest reactivity scores — meaning they were most relaxed — with their dogs and the highest with their spouses.[12]

Allen speculates that married couples might be able to reduce stress in their marital relationship by having an animal companion. She also discovered that couples with pets enjoyed greater closeness and satisfaction in marriage than those without. The more individuals were attached to their pets, the more likely they were to report frequent and positive interactions with their spouses.[13]

Animals help heal people in any number of situations. A program allowing women in prison to train companion dogs for the elderly both lessened depression and increased self-esteem.[14] And men in prison who were given the responsibility of caring for a pet modified their violent behavior.[15]

By now many people are familiar with the sight of animals raising the spirits of nursing home residents. We have seen pictures of dogs snuggled in beds, rabbits cuddled in the laps of wheelchair-bound residents, and cats lying lazily in an octogenarian's arms. Studies describe many positive effects from such animal companionship: increased social interaction with peers, reduced heart rates, reduced need for medication, enhanced self-esteem, and improved morale among nursing home staff. The same benefits were derived from a pet-facilitated therapy project at a hospice.[16]

Without doubt, the evidence supporting animals' ability to heal us and keep us well is impressive. And while scientists can measure the physiological and psychological benefits of animal companionship, it is incontestable that the most important healing that animals give us is spiritual. First, both our physical and psychological health are intertwined with our spiritual well-being. Spiritual disciplines such as yoga understand that our relationship to our body, our breath, the food we eat, and the thoughts we have are all components of a spiritual path. By soothing our spirits and calming our bodies, animals heal us spiritually.

What is it about the human-animal relationship that makes this so? Much of spiritual longing is the aching desire to transcend the limitations of self and ego, to reach out and experience our place in a greater whole. We yearn to overcome the limitations of our bodies, our own narrow perspectives, and to discover the "all that is." We begin to realize that we are operating in a narrowed, reduced level of consciousness. We meditate, pray, practice yoga, and practice other disciplines as a way to expand our consciousness. We want to reach across that which divides us to dissolve boundaries.

This is what animals do for us. When we relate to them as "other," yet also as our kin, our fellow creatures of God and the universe, we enter an expanded level of consciousness. They guide us over the threshold between the "here" of our limited understanding of existence and the "there" of mystery and wonder.

And the Children Will Lead Us

Many animals exhibit an intense interest in children. They gravitate to them — acting as their protectors, lavishing affection and attention on them, and simply wanting to be near them. In his book *Next of Kin*, researcher Roger Fouts tells the moving story of Brownie, the dog who was a member of his family as a boy. Brownie sacrificed her life by throwing herself between Roger's brother, who was bicycling by the side of the road, and an oncoming truck.[17] Another account, which received attention in the national media, concerns a dog who fended off a deadly snake to save a young toddler in his family. Although the dog was bitten repeatedly, he successfully protected the young child. Miraculously, he also recovered from his snake bites.

Often dogs simply exhibit an unqualified enthusiasm for children. Jeffrey Masson described the passion — there is no other word for it — that one of his dogs, Sasha, has for young children. She cannot resist running up to any child and lavishing her with an enthusiastic, wet kiss on the face. Children who have been the recipients of Sasha's kisses invariably respond with delight: "That dog kissed me!"

Masson, puzzling over the significance of children to his child-loving dog, wonders, "Is there some hidden similarity that I have not yet uncovered between dogs and small children?" He muses that "perhaps it is the recognition that children and [Sasha] are somehow siblings — an acknowledgment of emotional similarity that is deeper than the recognition of specieshood."[18]

I think Masson would agree that the recognition of kinship — a recognition that crosses the species boundary — is mutual. Dogs, as well as children, sense that they share something fundamental and life-affirming: the capacity to express unfettered love and joy, to feel emotions spontaneously and guilelessly, and the ability to make themselves vulnerable — all necessary ingredients for our spiritual development. Animals can be significant participants and teachers in the moral and spiritual development of children.

At times animals become beguiled by children; they recognize that the human baby is different from the human adult and, like us, they are fascinated with the young of another species. Cathy, a woman who works with a pet-facilitated therapy community group, relates the story of her cockatiel, Rana, who fell in love with a visiting baby. Like many cockatiels, Rana has an impressive vocabulary of sixty words and phrases. One day Cathy agreed to watch her friend's two-month-old baby for a few hours. As soon as the baby arrived, Rana gravitated toward her. When Cathy placed the baby in her crib, Rana perched on the side of the crib and stared down at her, repeating "baby," "baby," "baby." Cathy also noticed that when Rana spoke the word "baby" he employed "code switching," the adjustment of a word's tone and cadence to suit the context. Rana spoke the word "baby" in a high, sing-song voice different from his usual voice. Rana used the same voice a human adult would use when approaching an infant. Bird and baby remained enthralled with one another until the mother came to retrieve her daughter. Cathy wondered where Rana had learned the word "baby" since she had never taught it to him. The only explanation she could come up with was that Rana had once known a kitten named "Baby," and through familiarity with the young of one species could recognize the young of another.

Children also experience a natural affinity for animals — an interest that researchers find begins in infancy. As a species we seem to understand this intuitively: we fill children's lives with animal presences — through books, art, and videos. The stuffed ones are cuddled, named, and become trusted confidants. The plastic ones accompany them in their baths, floating in the tub. Most children learn to count by counting animals and they learn to read from pages adorned with pictures of animals.

There are, of course, real animals in their lives: companions at home and creatures encountered in nature. Eugene Myers, who documents the way in which animals influence children's moral and social development in his book *Children and Animals*, proposes that "children's relations to animals tap processes that lie deep in our own human animality and that bind us not only to each other but also to other species."[19] And the late ecopsychologist Paul Shepard contends that animals have played an integral role in the development of human intelligence. Our involvement with animals, he proposed, influences learning processes in children and social relations among adults.[20]

Children's interest in animals is passionate, uncensored, and unself-conscious. We as adults can only envy the degree to which children spontaneously identify with animals, an identification that facilitates their ethical development. And the point of ethical understanding "is to understand and promote the intimate relations that connect us with others and God."[21] Writer and publisher Jon Wynne-Tyson's recollection of a childhood experience demonstrates this connection. One evening as he was preparing for bed, he became disturbed when his mother killed some mosquitoes. The next morning, recounting the mosquitoes' deaths, he objected to his mother, noting that the mosquitoes had "been playing with their little friends and we go and kill them." She responded that the mosquitoes had to be killed because they were by nature so unkind. Without pause, he responded, "Yes, but what about 'love your enemies'?"[22]

Another young boy insisted that a monkey brought in by his keeper to his preschool class could understand English because "he's related to us."[23] His declaration revealed a grasp of essential lessons about evolution and the unity of life. And a young girl I recently overheard at a market counter while I waited to place my order also exhibited a spontaneous identification with her animal kin. On the lower shelves in front of the counter were a variety of items. One was a fish; the top and bottom third of the fish were gone. Now wrapped in plastic, only the middle section remained, framed by rough red edges where the other parts of the fish had been cut away. The young girl, probably about eight years old, was standing next to me, her mother to her right. She looked down at the fish, and exclaimed with great distress, "Mommy, mommy, look at that poor fish! Look at that fish! What happened to it?" Her mother tried to distract her, but the little girl would not be distracted. She continued to express her concern about the fate and condition of the fish.

We may smile with amusement when a child expresses concern for a mosquito's well-being, claims that a monkey can understand human language, or expresses concern for the fate of a fish. But these children are practicing empathic identification — an essential spiritual exercise. This identification bridges differences and focuses on the continuities of existence, rather than the discontinuities. Although we must acknowledge discontinuity, categorization, and difference as we conduct our daily professional and personal lives, they are not conducive to spiritual understanding.

Animals are significant, living beings in children's lives. Children do not experience them as abstractions or symbols. Adults may relegate animals to the periphery of their attention — but not children. What we sometimes call "innocence" in children is actually unspoiled wisdom. Children are untainted by cultural prejudices created by the fear of otherness. They are free of social protocol that dismisses or demeans the position of animals in our lives. To children, animals are not lower — they are fellow beings of equal standing, worthy of the same treatment as a fellow human. One little boy, when asked by his parents what he liked about the turtles that had been brought to his preschool classroom, exclaimed: "They're real!" It is the very realness of animals, a realness paradoxically brought to life through how they differ from our human species, that contrasts with the virtual reality of the computer games and videos that inundate children's lives.

The central role that animals play in our lives does not, of course, have to change as we grow up. Perhaps we are influenced by cultural pressure to abandon our fascination with animals, a pressure that can be found in the messages of much of children's literature. The theologian Stephen Webb discovered that stories for children often teach that sacrifice of a beloved animal is a necessary step toward maturity. He observes, "The death of an animal marks the transition from an imagination that is unbounded and inclusive to a conceptual awareness of absolute difference and rigid hierarchies."[24] Yet it is these absolute differences and rigid hierarchies that block our spiritual progression. As adults we must engage in spiritual exercises to remove the obstacles we erected while growing up, so that we can comprehend once again the indivisibility of existence. We must reacquaint ourselves with the truth that most children already know — animals are our kin.

Love

Many wise people have used a great diversity of stories and words to describe spirituality. When we get down to the essence of spirituality, however, it is simply about love. As Martin Buber wrote, "If you wish to believe, love!"[25] If you wish to believe, to develop spiritually, to expand your consciousness, you need to love: fully, completely, unabashedly, joyfully.

Animals are experts on love. In the last twenty years, thanks to researchers like Jane Goodall, Roger Fouts, and Jeffrey Masson, we have learned more about animals — both those who live free and those with whom we share our lives — and their ability to love. One young chimp that Jane Goodall studied loved his mother so much that after she died he wasted away, eventually dying of grief.[26] Ally, another young chimp, would have died after his separation from his human mother, the only mother he had known, if it were not for the intervention of Roger Fouts and his assistant, Bill Chown. After Ally's human mother decided she could no longer look after him, she left him with a small colony of chimpanzees under the care and study of

Roger and Deborah Fouts and their graduate students. After the separation, Ally became despondent, pulling his hair out and losing the use of his right arm from hysterical paralysis. Fouts and Chown, fearing for Ally's life, carried him close to their chests wherever they went. They did this every waking minute, day after day; Ally was never alone. After two months of such loving care, Ally emerged from his depression and came back to life.[27]

Chimps, of course, are not the only animals capable of exceptional demonstrations of love. Masson describes an account of a group of elephants who lovingly and successfully rescued a young rhino caught in the mud, despite the attacks of nearby adult rhinos, who feared the elephants were trying to harm the youngster.[28]

And every day, we directly experience the love of the animals with whom we share our lives — love without reservation, judgment, or expectation. The animals by our side don't care what we look like, how successful we are, whether we are fat or thin, rich or poor. They simply love us. We benefit from their attention and enjoy their unconditional love, a love that never doubts our motives, neither wavering nor withdrawing.

Adult humans, on the other hand, complicate love. We tend to love ambivalently. Our love comes mixed with other emotions: lack of trust, fear of loss of control, hesitancy to expose our vulnerability, doubt, and a resistance to relinquishing our own self-interest. Animals can teach us about love, about becoming vulnerable, and about leaving doubt behind.

Love has many aspects; the capacity to trust is one of them. The lessons animals teach us about trust are not abstract or symbolic but concrete and dramatic. A neighbor and friend of mine, Judy Johnson, once told me about an experience she had at Harper's Ferry, West Virginia, immediately after a hurricane. She and a small group of people stood on a bridge marveling at the frightening power of the swollen, surging Potomac and Shenandoah Rivers below.

A young woman with her golden retriever stood on the bank of one of the rivers near the bridge. Unthinkingly, she picked up a stick and threw it into the water for her dog to fetch. The dog swam for the stick, but quickly became overwhelmed by the surging current. Everybody looked on in horror as the dog was swept away. The current thrust him against a large boulder, to which he clung desperately. At first, the onlookers breathed a sigh of relief when they saw the dog reach the rock. But his reprieve from danger was short-lived.

The currents continued to push against the dog. He would lose his grip, struggle, and barely find another part of the rock to grasp. The young woman frantically called for him to swim toward her. He would try, but it was physically impossible to swim against the current. The swift movement of the river would carry him back to where he had started, clinging to the rock for safety. Everybody could see the dog growing weaker.

Looking around, Judy noticed the currents of the rivers met at a point downstream. She yelled to the young woman to run across the bridge to the other side of the river, to stand at the convergence and call her dog. She ran to the point, which stood behind her dog, and called to him. The dog looked over his shoulder as he heard her call. Without hesitation, he let go of the rock, and as he did, the current swept him to safety, where he was reunited with his human companion.

Could any of us trust as that dog did? It is certainly one of my spiritual aspirations. The golden retriever's trust for his companion came from the ability of dogs to love without hesitation or doubt. Love allowed the golden retriever to let go.

Many spiritual practices aim at helping practitioners to let go. To advance spiritually, we need to relinquish control, to move beyond our ego. We need to realize that there are no guarantees in life and no material permanence. Until we let go, our vision of the vast web of creation is obscured — by fear, desire, and any number of emotions separating us from the unity of existence.

Michael, a man who acknowledges that he has difficulty accepting loss, received inspiration from his dog, Daisy. Michael was aware that in his relationships he erected barriers between himself and other people, barriers meant to protect him from loss. He had learned the lesson that if one loves, eventually one will also suffer loss. No one can guarantee that a relationship will survive until death; and even if it does, we still die. Michael sensed he was holding back, and his partner sensed it, too. He was unsatisfied with the limitations he put on his love, yet he couldn't overcome his fear of loss. That is until Daisy, with her devoted, unwavering, boundless love for Michael, taught him how to love. Daisy's love pierced the barriers Michael had erected. He was able to learn to love without defending himself. Knowing that dogs live, depending on their size and other factors, from ten to fifteen years, Michael was constantly aware that one day Daisy would die. The fear aroused by this knowledge, however, withered in the face of Daisy's love. In time, Michael brought the open-hearted love that Daisy had taught him to his other relationships — with his wife, mother, and close friends.

Not only can animals teach us about trust, they also can teach us to transcend our self-interest. Bud, a cat, an exemplar of such selflessness, had an event-filled life. As a young kitten, Bud was rescued by Judy Johnson and her daughter, Samantha. Bud needed rescuing. He was flea-ridden, weak, and sick. As he grew stronger and began to thrive, Judy noticed that of all her cats Bud appeared to be the most attached to his home. He loved being at home — and no wonder. Home was where he had found life through the tender care of his human friends.

When Bud was about a year old, his home suffered a devastating fire. Samantha, who was in the house when the fire started, looked for the cats as she made her escape. Most of them appeared to have fled.

After the fire, Judy and Samantha started searching for their cats, scraping through the rubble the fire had left. Under the deck, atop a smoldering pile of wood, they found Bud perched, blackened, smelling like gasoline, but unhurt. Unlike Judy's other cats, Bud had refused to leave his home, against all reason.

Judy rebuilt her house, and life began to return to normal. The trauma of the fire receded. Bud went on with his life in the home he loved. A few years after the fire, Maggie, one of Judy's neighbors and friends, came to tell Judy that her long-ailing husband, Carl, had died the day before. As they were talking and grieving together, Bud crawled up into Maggie's lap, where he remained. When Maggie got up to return home, Bud followed her, never to return to Judy's again. From that night on he made his home with Maggie, with the mutual consent of both Maggie and Judy.

Bud, of course, couldn't replace Maggie's husband, Carl. But Bud brought a new life into the house that lifted Maggie's spirits and filled her days with love.

How do we explain Bud's actions? I don't pretend to understand his motivation. I do know that he gave up a home he loved and filled Maggie's home with affection and companionship that was welcome and healing.

There really is no adequate way to explain love. This is not a failure, but rather a statement about its nature. We intuit and experience love, rather than know it rationally. It is the stuff of poetry, not prose; of mystery, not certainty. Love, like all that is sacred and holy, cannot be categorized, dissected, or ever completely penetrated by rational, conscious methods. Trying to grasp love with words is futile and can lead us away from it. Animals simply live love. With their help, we can, too.

Chapter Two

Entering a Spiritual
Relationship with Animals

The Two Pillars of Awareness and Compassion

There is a well-known parable about the man searching for his keys at night under the light of a lamppost. Bent over, eyes glued to the ground, he carefully covers every inch of the lighted area without finding his keys. Of course, the keys lie just beyond the lighted area, in the dark, but visible if he would just look beyond the obvious.

This is a lesson about awareness. Awareness concerns seeing in a new way, suddenly seeing what was right before us yet we failed to see. For example, my sister, Carole, and I discussed the successful efforts of animal rights organizations to end the practice of releasing doves at the end of an Olympic ceremony. The dramatic symbolism of hundreds of doves ascending into the sky can be very moving. Carole remembered that she had liked watching that part of the ceremony without thinking, as few of us did, about the doves' experience. At that level of awareness, we saw the doves as interesting objects providing dramatic currency, but we were ignoring their subjective experience. It simply didn't enter our thoughts. The doves, of course, were frightened, confused, and disorganized after being crowded underground for who knows how long and then propelled upward.

The Olympics, to their credit, ended the practice, but it continues in other places. Carole's memory of the Olympic doves was rekindled by her trip to Disneyland, where the custom persists. This time my sister observed the doves more closely and began to notice what was happening to them. She noticed some faltering or flying off in a wrong direction. She could see their confusion, and resolved to write Disneyland about this practice.

Carole's awareness had changed. She now saw more deeply. This example supports an important principle: The "key" we all yearn for, the key that will help us participate in the wonder of creation and feel a sense of the interconnectedness of life, is before us, within our reach. Perhaps it is not directly under the lamppost, but it is visible if we just look.

How was my sister able to see more deeply — to truly pay attention to what was happening to the doves? I believe there is no easy way to expand our awareness. But, while it is not easy, it is possible. To begin with, Carole had taken many steps before reaching this insight. She has always loved animals; as children we had companion animals who were members of the family. When she married, we had a brief discussion over the "custody" of our beloved boxer, Monte. My sister knew she wouldn't take Monte with her when she moved out West with her husband, but she couldn't help asking.

Throughout her adult life Carole has collected photographs and paintings of animals; elephants and tigers are favorites. Her collection is one manifestation of her curiosity about and appreciation for the animals that she has encountered in her travels throughout the world. For the last few years she has volunteered at her local humane society, an undertaking that not only entails a time commitment but a willingness to end her Saturdays dusty and with sore muscles from exercising enthusiastic, and very grateful, dogs.

My sister's growing sensitivity to the treatment of animals also occurred in the context of our relationship. As I became more aware about the position of animals in our world, I would share my new-found information with Carole. Together we inquired, learned, and began to see more. Her example points to an important principle: *Awareness occurs in a relationship or a context.*

I have previously written about my belief that "the fundamental reality is one of relatedness."[1] As a psychologist I know the psychological importance of relationships, and the paradox that the self only exists through relationship with others. The person we know as "self" only comes into being through intimate relationships.

Our earliest relationships shape how we see ourselves and others, and influence our interactions in future relationships. Some people, for example, appear to have an inborn confidence in their abilities. They have a realistic appraisal of what they can accomplish, and they are often willing to take on new challenges.

The confidence these people radiate isn't necessarily inborn, however. One way individuals achieve this confidence is when their parents perceive them as capable and effective and consistently expose them to experiences appropriate to their developmental level. Through these experiences children learn to exercise their judgment and improve their abilities.

What was at first the parents' view of the child becomes the child's view of self. And then, feeling self-confident, he succeeds, which builds confidence — and confidence builds more confidence. As a child goes out into the world and meets others, he assumes that others will view him as his parents do — as a competent and reliable person. All of these experiences reinforce and deepen the child's sense of confidence.

Of course, not all children have parents who are able to convey this sense to a child. Fortunately, it is not just our earliest relationships that form us, although they certainly are crucial. Relationships continue to form us throughout our lives. Teachers, peers, friends, and partners can all play substantial roles in our development. The field of psychology has firmly established the importance of relationships not only to our growth and development, but also to our current functioning.[2] By now, most of us are familiar with this idea and accept it.

A corollary to the importance of relationships to our psychological functioning is the spiritual concept of relatedness, or interconnectedness. This relatedness or interconnectedness has been characterized as a "web of existence," which, when we enter it, helps us to recognize that we are a part of a larger whole. One compelling and well-known image of this "web of existence" comes from Buddhism. Francis Cook, a scholar of Hua-yen Buddhism, tells it like this: In the heavenly abode of the great god Indra there is a spectacular net, hung by some cunning artisan, so that it stretches out in all directions, into infinity. The artisan has hung a single glittering jewel in each "eye" of the net. Since the net is infinite, the jewels are infinite in number. "There hang the jewels, glittering like stars of the first magnitude, a wonderful sight to behold. If we now arbitrarily select one of these jewels for inspection and look closely at it, we will discover that in its polished surface there are reflected *all* the other jewels in the net, infinite in number. Not only that, but each of the jewels reflected in this one jewel is also reflecting all the other jewels, so that there is an infinite reflecting process occurring." The story of Indra's net paints a vivid picture of the dynamic interrelatedness of all creation.[3]

Through awareness, we become able to transcend our own individual particularity and to unite with the other. Sometimes the other is another human being; sometimes the other is God. A sense of communion also can be achieved through a realization of the nonduality of existence, so that the distinction between self and other is transcended. Instead of distinctions, one encounters a vast emptiness, symbolized by the Chinese character *ku*, which, as writer and Zen teacher Peter Matthiessen explains, "also signifies the clear blue firmament, without north or south, future or past, without boundaries or dimension." He continues, "Ku contains all forms....Thus this emptiness is also fullness, containing all forms and phenomena above and below Heaven, filling the entire universe."[4] Whether in uniting with the other that other is another earthly being, God, or the recognition of nonduality, this connection cannot be achieved without awareness.

We can return to the example of my sister, Carole, to develop another aspect of awareness: *Awareness requires our attention and action.* It isn't about something miraculous happening to us. Awareness is about deciding, learning, and acting. Carole was able to expand her awareness of the doves' plight, and thereby gain an experience of her relationship to the "web of existence," because she was paying attention. She paid attention through her appreciation and curiosity about animals, through her work at the humane society, by reading, and in her conversations with me.

Most important, she was paying attention by looking beyond the lighted area — by considering ideas, perceptions, and feelings that were outside of her usual thinking.

Georg Feuerstein, author of numerous books and a leader in the field of yoga, writes that all spiritual traditions of the world have a similar goal, "Waking up from the dream that we call the waking state." Enlightenment only comes when we break through the stupor of our conditioned patterns of thinking and responding and begin to apply "intensified attention or mindfulness." Feuerstein correctly proposes that waking up "calls for a deliberate act of will."[5]

Beyond action, *awareness is also about love and a loving receptivity.* But what does it mean to love in this sense? This love does not refer to romantic love, or brotherly love, or the love of God for humankind. When referring to human forms of love, these types of love emphasize individual relationships. In the context of spiritual awareness, however, the character of love may take on another definition. The type of love described by mystics and religious teachers intends to take in the fullness of the other with wonder and appreciation and without drawing distinctions that separate us from the other. Most significant, this love may be directed at the *whole* of creation, not just at an individual. This love is all-embracing, and in its embrace we achieve a union with existence itself.

Love demands that we stretch ourselves beyond our usual way of thinking, often characterized by defining ourselves by our differences. Sometimes the difference we find is gender or race. Other times it is religion or nationality. As the human race has matured, we have begun to realize that organizing ourselves by these differences not only disenfranchises others but also diminishes us. But even as we find unity within the human race, we still go to great lengths to distinguish ourselves from other species. We need to extend our care and understanding to all species, and to accept the invitation of Christian theologian Jay McDaniel "[to] be life-centered...to live out a sense of kinship with all of life, not human life alone."[6]

Awareness makes one more demand on us: that we use our awareness on the behalf of others. *Awareness is not an end in itself; it is also the source of compassion. Reciprocally, compassion is necessary to complete awareness.*

Compassion is the underlying principle of the Golden Rule and, for Buddhists, it is the path to enlightenment.[7] Crucial to the notion of compassion is the ability to see the other's suffering and then to respond to it; compassion requires us to take action that will relieve suffering. It makes us moral agents.

The activities of awareness and compassion not only shape our spiritual development, they also build our character. For example, Buddhism, with its system of karma and reincarnation, has the concept of the Bodhisattva.[8] A Bodhisattva is an individual who has achieved a state of full enlightenment (which would take many lifetimes), and in achieving this state is capable of leaving behind the world of suffering. Instead, the Bodhisattva chooses to stay in the world of suffering and endless rebirth *(samsara)* in order to help others reach enlightenment. Inspired by the Bodhisattva ideal, the "engaged Buddhism" movement now "tak[es] to heart the Bodhisattva vow to save all beings" by actively working for social justice and peace.[9]

It is through ethical action, based on spiritual insight, that character is formed. We are what we do. The concept of the interweaving of action with spiritual growth, and the relationship between spiritual action and personal character, perhaps is captured best by the poem found in the Buddhist text *Anguttara Nikaya*, as quoted by Joanna Macy:

> My action is my possession,
> my action is my inheritance,
> my action is the womb which bears me,
> my action is my refuge.[10]

Compassion, then, is an action. It also is a strong feeling, not a sentiment, which trivializes it. Compassion requires, and is linked etymologically and essentially to, passion. Compassion is to feel passionately with and about another. It is to be fully engaged with their sorrow, rage, joy, or ecstasy. It is to participate in the suffering of another, and also to join in their celebrations.

Compassion is a kind of "fierce tenderness" that contains a powerful energy. It is the energy of a fierce warrior determined to relieve suffering. Compassion requires an ability to open oneself to the other's experience, to feel strongly and deeply, and then to act resolutely.

Operating in concert, awareness and compassion develop our capacity to experience an essential understanding of another; they guide us to experience the intricately magnificent interrelatedness of all of creation, and inform our actions for the other. Informed by awareness and compassion, we are able to see the other in a new light. It is a knowing of the other unmediated by distinctions — the barriers of sex, race, or species.

The movement, then, is a dynamic interplay between increased awareness and compassionate action. It is a movement that goes through the ups and downs of any spiritual process. These are the two activities — awareness and compassion — that are essential to our spiritual development.

Ultimately, it is our pursuit of awareness and compassion that takes us down the path toward grace.

Suffering and Spiritual Growth

When I was a young girl, and our family would take a long-distance road trip, sometimes we would break from our travels by stopping for various forms of animal entertainment. On our family trips to Florida, we would pile out of the hot and dusty car and buy our tickets to watch a young man "wrestle" an alligator. These wrestling matches were always billed as exotic, death-defying battles, but as far as I could tell the man always won.

The pony ride was another roadside attraction. Whenever my sister and I spotted one, we would voice our enthusiastic desire — in high-pitched children's voices — to stop for the ride. My father, who often accommodated his children, would usually stop. Neither my sister, nor me, nor my parents gave any thought to the condition of the ponies. We thought only about our fascination for these gentle animals. Today, of course, we are more aware that animals, too, live in the world as we do, and have needs, interests, desires, and preferences. In other words, we are more aware of what it is like to be the animal ridden by children or wrestled by young men. Was that alligator drugged? Probably. Alligators are not made to wrestle human beings, so whatever was done to ensure that the man consistently won the wrestling match could not have been good for the alligator.

Was the pony given comfortable quarters, kept cool, well watered and fed? I hope so; but maybe not. I do recall that the ponies behaved like automatons, without personality or life — probably an indication of distress.

Sometimes we are nudged to deeper awareness by a chance encounter. Animal advocate Betsy Swart tells the story of a Chimp Farm a roadside zoo in Florida that housed chimps in long rows of cages. It is one of the more than 1,200 roadside zoos that exist across the United States. Chimpanzees are highly intelligent, social animals, yet they were caged in isolation, with no room for exercise, no bedding on which to sleep, and for some, only minimal shelter from the weather.

A woman with her children stood in front of one of the cages where, despite the children's laughter and their jumping up and down, the chimp quietly rocked back and forth, hitting his head very softly against the wall of the concrete cage. Betsy, who visited the Chimp Farm to document the condition of the chimpanzees, asked the woman, "Do you think these animals are happy?" Annoyed at the question, the woman responded, "What kind of question is that? They're only animals." With that, she turned on her heel and she and her children began their tour.

What did they see on their tour? They encountered a baby chimp who spends his days pacing and banging his head on the walls of his Plexiglas prison. Periodically he would put his head against the Plexiglas, attempting to make contact with the head of a child on the outside. He sought touch, companionship, attachment, all of which he had been denied. Then they saw Konga, born in 1948, who still has an unremovable chain around his neck.Konga had been taught to simulate boxing, and the chain was used to control his movements. In additional cages were Johnnie, Rosie, and other chimps, all with sad stories. They paced back and forth, or rocked themselves for comfort. Other chimps, more seriously disturbed, paced, or bit themselves, or rattled their cages. Others threw food and feces at the tourists. One had given up, lying in a prenatal position with her eyes open. No amount of taunting or tossing of food would arouse her.

As Betsy Swart and her companions were leaving the Chimp Farm, the woman approached her and said, "You know, you were right....These animals aren't happy. They look like mental patients. I won't be coming back."[11]

We don't know what this woman did with her increased awareness. We do know that she became aware of their suffering. And with that initial awareness, she gained a spiritual opportunity that might lead to her own experience of grace. We may thirst for the spiritual expertise of the mystic who can "taste" God, or yearn for the enlightenment experience of the dedicated meditator, but we must remember that the path to spiritual wholeness often *begins with the invitation to become aware of suffering.*

In the Yoga tradition of Patanjali, becoming aware of the suffering of others is a necessary step in the path toward realization. Because pity, or compassion, is an unselfish emotion, it helps free us from our egos, and the limitations our egos place on us. In Swami Prabhavananda's words, "We may suffer deeply when we see others suffering, but our pity will teach us understanding — and hence freedom." [12]

To become aware of another's suffering we must expose ourselves to it. This entails stripping off our usual self-protective devices to take in the other's anguish. We must avoid rationalizations, such as "They don't know what's happening to them," or "They're probably out of it anyway when they are being slaughtered," or "They must give them a lot of anesthetic before they use them for research or testing."

Sometimes the animals know all too well what is happening to them. Often, for example, a dog or rat who undergoes experimental surgery may, or may not, be given an anesthetic, but, if given, frequently the anesthesia is poorly administered. Conducting an ethnographic study of research laboratories, sociologist Mary Phillips observed a postdoctoral fellow as he drilled into a rat's skull. The rat immediately began to squirm and struggle, his hind legs moving in a running motion. In a short time the rat's hind legs were hanging off the operating platform, but his head was held in place by a surgical device. "The researcher kept on working on the skull, paying no attention to the rat's frantic struggles," Phillips reports. The researcher asked for more anesthesia when the rat managed to kick over the platform, making it impossible for the operation to continue. "They all acted as though nothing unusual or untoward was going on," Phillips noted. [13]

She also discovered that animals are rarely administered analgesics after surgery, a finding confirmed by other researchers. [14] When she interviewed scientists about their use of animals for experimentation, many of them had never thought to administer an analgesic, even to a monkey after head surgery. Some expressed concern that an analgesic would interfere with their research results. Others had inaccurate physiological and/or pharmacological information concerning the appropriateness of giving analgesics.[15]

Research scientists are not consciously cruel. When they see an animal in a laboratory, however, they often do not let themselves see the animal as a living, feeling being who can suffer. Instead, they see a scientific object; whatever suffering and death is involved is justified, for "the animal is a 'sacrifice' on the altar of science."[16] While many of these researchers love and care for their own pets, Phillips notes that they see their pets as individuals with names. The animals they use in their laboratories are nameless, "de-individualized creatures, whose sole purpose in life [is] to serve in a scientific experiment."[17] The researchers have willfully limited their awareness in order to pursue science, which they believe — incorrectly — requires experimenting on animals.

But researchers are not always successful in blocking out the individuality of the animal they are using, especially when the animal forms an attachment to them. This was the case for a young medical student, as reported by the philosopher Tom Regan, who was his roommate at the time:

A determined student, Regan's roommate was assigned a dog in his surgery class on whom he would learn a variety of procedures. "He described to me how he broke the poor animal's leg and then set it, only to break it again and set it again," Regan writes. "Throughout her long, painful ordeal, the loyal animal greeted his arrival with a wag of her tail and even licked the very hands that had injured her. In the end, after he had studied one or another thing about her treatment and recovery, he was required to 'euthanize' the dog. It did not sit well with him. He thought it cruel and unnecessary. He wanted to speak out, to object, but he lacked the courage. He wondered what sort of human being he was or would become."[18] The dog's affection broke through the defenses the young medical student had developed to block his awareness; he became all too aware of her suffering. Regrettably we don't know if the medical student's new awareness resulted in any further action. We do know that spiritual development rests on the two pillars of awareness and compassion. Awareness initiates compassionate action, and compassion completes and deepens awareness.

It should go without saying that animals can and do suffer, except that for many years we have been led to believe otherwise. Descartes, who proposed that animals are like machines, declared that the cries of animals in laboratories are simply the equivalent to the noise a clock makes when ticking. Even today there are philosophers who insist, despite an abundance of evidence to the contrary, that animals are incapable of suffering. With the scientific information we have now about animals' lives, we know beyond a doubt that they think and suffer and feel. Mammals are all very similar neurophysiologically; we share a limbic system and a hypothalamus, both of which are involved in the experiences of positive and negative emotions, and our nervous systems contain the same biochemicals associated with pain.[19] Summarizing the growing body of research on animals, Donald Griffin, a researcher on animal behavior at Harvard, has written: "Animal feelings, and especially animal suffering, are recognized by most scientists as real and significant."[20]

Too often their suffering is unnecessary. Faced with suffering we can address, our job is to respond. Suffering calls out for our compassionate action. Carol Adams, a feminist writer and activist who writes about animal care, ecology, and ethics, concludes that it is "attention to suffering [that] makes us ethically responsible."[21]

I have been emphasizing the pervasive and needless animal suffering that surrounds our lives. It is suffering, and our response to it, that is an organizing concept for one school of moral philosophy represented by Peter Singer. He asks us "to consider our attitudes from the point of view of those who suffer by them, and by the practices that follow from them."[22]

Singer, who stresses the bedrock moral principle of equality, with an equal consideration of interests, takes the next step to extend it to animals. His central argument, first articulated by Jeremy Bentham over a century ago, is "The question is not, Can they *reason?* Can they *talk?* but, Can they *suffer?*"

Just as all humans are capable of suffering, whatever their mental ability, so are all animals — human and nonhuman. The right to equal consideration is based on the capacity to suffer; it is this vital characteristic that is the moral entry point, and the deciding factor in who deserves our sympathy and our compassionate action.

Sympathy is not only crucial to our ethical decision-making, it also is linked to loving. Charles Hartshorne, a process theologian, makes a case that God's power comes simply from "the appeal of unsurpassable love." By unsurpassable love, Hartshorne means God's unlimited capacity to feel sympathy for other creatures.[23] None of us, of course, can attain these God-like capacities; but the idea of God, and of God's unsurpassable love, can keep us moving, always moving, toward love.

It is never easy to think about these animals' experiences. As illustrated by the young medical student, the experience can be profoundly affecting. Most of us do not realize exactly what goes on behind the closed doors of research laboratories. It is well hidden from our view. But even when information is available to us, we may self-protectively prevent ourselves from fully entering the experience of the caged animals. We protect ourselves from being overwhelmed; acknowledging such suffering, we fear, would have fundamental implications for how we lead our lives. But the price we pay for this self-protection is the restriction of our spiritual growth.

To absorb the extent and depravity of animal suffering can raise us to a new spiritual level. This is the price of the ticket for animal grace. Our expanding awareness may lead us to feel that we are experiencing disorganization of the self, a significant price. Writer Joanna Macy teaches us, however, that what feels like a disintegration of the self in these periods of intense transformation is not the self breaking down but its defenses.[24] The breakdown of these defenses needs to be welcomed rather than feared, for they have dimmed our awareness and stunted our compassion. Their dissolution can free us spiritually. A commitment to spiritual growth, then, is a commitment to one's personal disarmament! The structure of the old defensive self must die so that a new, larger, and more encompassing structure can be born.

The Everydayness of a Spiritual Relationship with Animals

Paraphrasing Martin Buber, one way to believe and to love is to accept the gift of a spiritual relationship with animals. The intertwining of our lives with those of so many animals makes spirituality an active possibility at any moment of any day. A simple trip to the grocery store can be transformed from a meaningless chore into a spiritual process. Instead of merely walking down the aisles with our checklist, absentmindedly fingering fruit and daydreaming about a planned vacation, we have an opportunity to bring intention and care to this activity — and to every activity.

With such intention this seemingly mundane chore is transfigured. It becomes a celebration of life in which, with your actions, you honor the life that surrounds yours, and join that life in reverence. One way to do this is simply to make a commitment only to buy household products that have not been tested on animals. You do so because you have had the courage to open yourself to the suffering of the animals who have been used in this way. You have not turned your back or closed your mind out of fear or disinterest. You have listened and heard, and now you can respond with compassionate care.

With deep awareness, one can dedicate a moment to all animals who have unnecessarily suffered, acknowledge their sacrifice, and offer a commitment through one's actions to never again cause the unnecessary suffering of another animal. These moments, when practiced with consciousness, can be times when one enters a profound reverence for the sanctity of life. They are moments of grace. This grace can be experienced, right there, in the aisles of your supermarket. In turning your awareness and love toward animals, they offer you this remarkable gift of grace.

Many others have described the opportunity to find the sacred in the stream of everyday living. Most recently, the author Thomas Moore has awakened us to our daily opportunities to "enter a different level of experience." He invites us to find "an enchanted world...that speaks to the soul, to the mysterious depths of the heart and the imagination where we find value, love, and union with the world around us."[25] He is, I believe, using a different vocabulary to describe the same thing: bringing enchantment to your life means living a life of awareness, committed to compassionate action. Awareness and enchantment are discovered in the everyday by ordinary people.

Sometimes the ability to find enchantment in the world around you comes at an early age. The veterinarian, writer, and animal rights advocate Michael Fox, like many others, opened his mind and heart to nature at a young age. "Like the child in Walt Whitman's poem who went out into the world and became all that he perceived," he writes, "I entered the mystical world of nature...and became a part of everything....To play with a pond — and by that I mean to examine at close hand, to 'mind' everything that I perceived in it, on it, and around it — was to experience the miraculous."[26]

Children, in their seeming innocence, often see what we no longer can. It isn't so much that children have something adults don't, but that adults lose it along the way. Listening to children is one way to recover that which has been lost. For example, it is fairly common for children at some point to question how the food made its way to your home's table. When they realize that an animal was killed for this purpose, many are horrified and want no part of it. They react with a basic moral revulsion when they realize that another being's life was taken. These aspiring vegetarians, however, usually encounter stiff resistance from their parents and peers and learn to stifle their compassionate response. When they become adults, they may revisit this knowledge and embrace vegetarianism.

Not all parents react negatively when their children express an interest in eating food that does not involve killing a sentient being. For some it is the beginning of a spiritual path on which the whole family eventually embarks. One woman I know who is active in the animal rights movement was introduced to the plight of animals by her two daughters. At ages seven and nine, they stated their preference for a vegetarian diet after learning that animals were slaughtered for food. At first she tried to encourage them to continue eating meat — but not for long. Listening more carefully, she began to join them in their thinking. They all began to read more about vegetarianism, which led them to learn about the condition and treatment of animals in modern society. Mother and daughters learned together, and they committed as a family to honoring life. They walked down a spiritual path together.

Another friend remarked on the freedom and joy she has felt in her cooking since she became a vegetarian. She had learned the art of fine cooking and eating from her mother, but her culinary experience took on another dimension after she embraced vegetarianism. Her cooking became more than an art. It also became a life-giving, joyful experience filled with light. Now, she says, there is only life — and all of the swirling colors, textures, tastes, and richness of life. Cooking for her has become a time to reconnect to the spirit and to experience a moment of grace.

The spiritual possibilities of our relationships with animals fill our days — in trips to the grocery store, in selecting personal care products, in cooking our food. As we become more aware of this spiritual reality, we realize how animals surround and pervade our lives.

We are in relationship with animals in so many ways. Growing awareness requires that we consider the terms of that relationship. We can redefine our relationship so as to end all of the needless suffering of animals who are used to test cosmetics or medicine, or who become antibiotic- and hormone-ridden food after unbearable confinement in the endless crates of factory farms. We can say "no" to participating in that kind of relationship. More than saying "no" we are declaring an even more resounding "*yes!*" It is a *yes* to life and to the incredible wonder of creation. It is a *yes* to falling in love with the world around us — to becoming enchanted by the unity of existence.

In the fairy tales of my childhood, enchantment usually occurred while walking through the forest, when some magical figure would cast a spell on you. Enchantment, however, does not just happen to us. Rather, enchantment happens as a result of our intention to be aware, open, and receptive to the other. And, then, with that openness toward the other, we are drawn into an experience of the fullness of life. That is enchantment — to marvel at the joy and beauty and wonder of life. And enchantment comes from knowing that we are doing all we can to contribute to life and not to destruction.

The everydayness of a spiritual relationship to animals is a path to enchantment. It is the path of mystics, but mystics are not different from any one of us. The theologian Carol Ochs, in examining the lives and messages of mystics, found that the struggles of our daily life and the heroic struggles of the mystics are one and the same.[27] Any of us can lead a heroic life; we are each ordinary, and yet we also have the extraordinary potential to become mystics.

Amazing Grace

One such ordinary, yet incredible, person was John Newton. Like many in his day, Newton participated in the great evil of slavery, as the captain of a slave ship. A self-described "infidel" and "libertine," he led a profligate life, without spiritual direction. That is, until one night, when Newton's slave ship encountered a terrific storm in the middle of the Atlantic. Everyone on board, including Newton, scrambled to try to save the ship and themselves. True to character, Newton hurled defiant curses as they lost the battle. About to be overwhelmed by the sea's surging power, and beyond desperation, Newton sat in his cabin to await his fate. As he did, he heard himself say, "Lord have mercy upon us." Even with everything on his mind, he could not miss the significance of his words: Why was he appealing to a God he didn't think he believed in, a God he habitually dismissed with his curses? After Newton and his ship survived the storm, he began to consider his spiritual existence. Feeling he had been touched by God's grace, Newton began a lifelong process of discovering his faith.

Although Newton participated unenthusiastically in the slave trade for a few more years, the grace he had experienced continued to work in his life. Eventually he realized that any involvement in slavery was "unlawful and wrong." Nine years after his initial encounter with grace, he became an Anglican priest, and in 1760, at the age of thirty-five, he became a curate in the parish of Olney, England. Remorseful for his part in slavery and yet joyful at overcoming his blinding ignorance, Newton was inspired to write what has become one of the best-known hymns in history, "Amazing Grace." Continuing along his spiritual path, Newton became an active antislavery advocate. His testimony and activism were influential in England's abolishment of slavery shortly before he died in 1807.

"Amazing Grace" has had an unaccountable effect on people from all backgrounds — its words and music seem to reach something in almost everyone who has heard them. Regardless of a person's religious beliefs or background, "Amazing Grace" touches the soul in a way that defies explanation.

One of the most memorable lines of "Amazing Grace" — "I was blind and now I see" — touches a soulful chord in many of us. It is true we often are "blind" to that which we need to see, *and* it is also true we can recover from our blindness. Hearing this phrase, we are simultaneously filled with a profound sense of hope, joy, and gratitude that we can be liberated from our ignorance. Grace — working through awareness and our compassionate response — can free us.

Chapter Three

The Peaceable *Kindom*

The peaceable kindom, as described by the prophet Isaiah, is an evocative story of a time when all of us — human and animal, prey and predator — will come together in peace and harmony. Cooperation will replace competition, peace will supplant war, and harmony will prevail over conflict.

The Peaceable *Kingdom* is the historical phrase for this concept. The term "kingdom," however, implies domination and hierarchy, a system nonhuman animals, and many human animals, have lived under for too long. The substituted phrase "kindom" captures the intention much better — a community of life, comprising individual beings who are related to one another.

The prophecy of the peaceable kindom, which has captured the imagination of prophets, poets, and artists throughout history, provides inspiration for our spiritual searching. Richard A. Young, a theologian and author of *Is God a Vegetarian?*, reminds us that the stories we tell give direction to our lives.[1] The stories we hear, and the symbols they transmit, open us to a future we can shape through our actions, step by step, in the present-becoming-future. Stories such as that of the peaceable kindom map our spiritual direction and supply meaning to our lives by encouraging us to imagine possibilities that we otherwise would not have envisioned. And as we imagine the more-that-is-possible, we advance spiritually.

Isaiah's account of a peaceable kindom is brief, yet powerful:

> The wolf shall live with the lamb, the leopard shall lie down with the kid, the calf and the lion and the fatling together, and a little child shall lead them. The cow and the bear shall graze, their young shall lie down together; and the lion shall eat straw like the ox. The nursing child shall play over the hole of the asp, and the weaned child shall put its hand on the adder's den. They will not hurt or destroy on all my holy mountain; for the earth will be full of the knowledge of the Lord as the waters cover the sea (Isaiah 11:6–9).

The peaceable kindom would return us to that time when the earth was "full of the knowledge of the Lord." This was a time of Edenic peace, as depicted in Genesis 1:29–30: "everything that has the breath of life, I have given every green plant for food."

J. R. Hyland, a theologian who has written on the biblical basis for the humane treatment of animals, describes the concept of "progressive revelation," as having to do "with the belief that although God's self-revelation does not change, the human capacity to receive that revelation does change. It grows and develops as people progress in their ability to understand who God is and what constitutes right relationship to the Creator."[2] Applying this perspective to the premonitions of the great prophets, she interprets this passage to indicate God's intention for a world filled with creatures living in harmony with one another, free from the concepts of predator and prey. She writes that God gives the same instructions to both human and nonhuman animals — to enjoy a nonviolent, vegetarian diet — because both groups share the same "breath of life." This biblical passage, Hyland asserts, clearly establishes God's intention for parity between human and nonhuman animals, as God's creatures are all loved and valued.

The prophets Isaiah, Jeremiah, and Hosea ushered in the prophetic age in Israel, a time also known as the "messianic age" and the "future hope of Israel." Their emergence signaled a significant shift in the spiritual journey of the Jewish people, one that influenced not just Jews but many others as well. They appeared at a time when violence, warfare, and corruption dominated much of life, with only brief interludes of spiritual progress. The world's inhabitants, for the most part, had turned their backs on the possibility of an earthly Eden.

The prophets' vision encompassed secular as well as spiritual concerns, emphasizing social justice, mercy, and compassion for all living creatures. They called upon their people to "beat their swords into plowshares" (Isa. 2:4) and reminded all not to "oppress the alien, the orphan or the widow" (Jer. 7:6).

With his prophecy, Hosea confirms Isaiah's vision of a peaceable kindom, foretelling of a time when humans will no longer kill animals:

> In that day I will make a covenant for them;
> With the beast of the field and the birds of the air
> And the creatures that move along the ground.
> Bow and sword and battle
> I will abolish from the land,
> So that all may lie down in safety (Hosea 2:18).

These great prophets did not introduce new concepts as much as they provided a crucial reminder to the Jewish people of the ideals recorded in the Hebrew Bible to guide them: love, compassion, justice, and mercy for all of God's creatures. The Prophetic Age, Hyland suggests, "signaled that it was time for the human race to remember its beginnings."[3]

The image of a peaceable kindom, like a beacon lighting our path, helps us find a way back to our spiritual origins. It returns us to the awareness that all life is sacred and interrelated, and that all living beings deserve our compassionate response. In turn, through awareness and compassion, we can find the peaceable kindom within ourselves.[4]

Modern-Day Versions of a Peaceable Kindom:
Little Tyke and Poplar Springs Animal Sanctuary

Is Isaiah's vision meant to be interpreted literally? Are carnivorous animals really meant to become vegetarian? Impossible, you say? Well, not quite. There is one confirmed case of a vegetarian lion, Little Tyke, the fifth cub of a mother who was taken from her natural habitat and placed in a zoo. The mother, driven to frenzied grief by her imprisonment, had killed Little Tyke's four older siblings before zookeepers could get near her. Although badly mauled, Little Tyke was rescued, and sent by zoo officials to live at Hidden Valley Ranch, the home of Georges and Margaret Westbeau.

The inhabitants of Hidden Valley — the lion cub, lambs, dogs, cats, chickens, and deer — lived in close contact with one another. When the cub first arrived, the Westbeaus assumed she would need meat in order to survive. Despite their attempts to provide it, often involving elaborate subterfuge, the lion cub refused all animal flesh. Eventually, after a conversation with an animal behaviorist, one of the many experts they had consulted, the Westbeaus relaxed and stopped forcing meat on her. The expert asked them if they read the Bible and referred them to Genesis 1:30, which reads, "And to every beast of the earth, and to every fowl of the air, and to everything that creepeth upon the earth, wherein there is life, I have given every green herb for meat: and it was so." The Westbeaus gladly acceded to Little Tyke's insistence on a vegetarian diet, a diet on which she thrived. Little Tyke did lay down with the calf, just as the prophet Isaiah had prophesied.[5]

I have not enjoyed the pleasure of seeing a lion and calf peacefully coexisting. But I have directly experienced another "peaceable kindom": Poplar Springs Animal Sanctuary, located less than an hour from my home in suburban Maryland.

Poplar Springs is one of the latest sanctuaries in the rapidly growing sanctuary movement, which started in the United States about twenty-five years ago and has grown dramatically in the past fifteen years. Although there is no official count, one expert estimates the U.S. has roughly 200 sanctuaries, not counting smaller operations run by individuals with their own funds. The Association of Sanctuaries, which began in 1992, however, is compiling a sanctuary database. They also are establishing sanctuary guidelines, instituting an accrediting process that would consider the quality of the enclosures, the stability of the organization, stimulating activities for the animals, and veterinary care. In addition, accreditation would require that the sanctuary not breed animals without approval from the U.S. Department of Interior's Species Survival Plan for endangered species. They also may not allow the animals to be used for any commercial purpose.

There are all manner of sanctuaries — for farm animals, chimpanzees, pelicans, elephants, big cats, pigs, horses, wildlife, and more. The inhabitants of Poplar Springs include cows, horses, pigs, goats, chickens, roosters, turkeys, wild geese, and ducks.

Terry Cummings and her husband, David Hoerauf, opened Poplar Springs in January 1997. I recently visited Poplar Springs, their 400-acre farm in Poolesville, Maryland, to meet Terry and David and many of the animals who live there. Unlatching the gate, and driving down the mile-long road to Terry and David's barns and house, you enter a different world. A sign on the gate makes it clear that no fishing or hunting is allowed within. All animals are safe from human predation beyond this point. The only noise you can hear is the sound of tires on gravel; the quiet introduces a feeling of calm, an anticipation that you are entering a unique environment.

Although Poplar Springs opened very recently, Terry and David's animal family is growing quickly. The latest infusion of residents made a dramatic, heartrending entrance. An eighteen-wheeler, packed with 171 pigs headed for slaughter, was abandoned on a busy street in Washington, D.C. It didn't take long for the D.C. police to discover the truck, with its terrified, squealing passengers.

The police contacted the Washington Humane Society and

members of animal protection groups rushed to the scene. After Terry and David were consulted, the truck, with all of the pigs inside, was towed to Poplar Springs. By the time it arrived, four pigs had died from the stress and heat of being crammed into small cages stacked three layers tall. Pigs do not sweat and it is difficult for them to regulate their body temperatures in close quarters. By the time they reached Poplar Springs they had been on the truck for at least fourteen hours.

The surviving 167 frightened pigs were helped off the truck. None of the pigs, who were between five and six months old, and already between 200 and 250 pounds, were in good shape. Many had urine burns on their backs from the pigs above them. David judged from their burns that the pigs had not just been confined to tiered crates for their voyage to the slaughterhouse but for their entire short lives on the factory farm. Their tails had been cut off, and all suffered from badly bruised and swollen legs.

Once off the truck, they weren't quite sure what to do. Having been confined to crates all their lives, none had ever walked, let alone on grass. They had never seen daylight or felt the sun. Breezes had never touched their skin. Confined to crates, they had never interacted with one another. Shy and hesitant at first, they began to walk with faltering steps. Within days, they were not only walking with greater assurance, they were scampering about, intermingling with one another, and learning to enjoy their freedom.

Twenty-two of the pigs stayed with Terry and David at Poplar Springs. The other 145 went to two other more established animal sanctuaries, Pigs A Sanctuary and Farm Sanctuary. Some of the pigs were permanently disabled by their life on the factory farm. One pig, Arnie, was lying in his stall when I saw him. Terry said he has such bad arthritis from his confinement that he cannot walk and can barely stand. There is hope for Arnie, though. He is on arthritis medication, which seems to be helping him. Terry is optimistic that with the medication he can have a reasonable quality of life.

Every animal at Poplar Springs — whether a pig, cow, horse, goat, sheep, turkey, or chicken — has her or his story. Each was abandoned, neglected, or abused before reaching the sanctuary. Chewy the lamb was found tied to a pole at a local shopping center. Cowvin started life as a veal calf. Too sick for auction, he collapsed and was thrown alive into a dumpster. Luckily, someone saw him and bought him for a dollar. Now he lives at Poplar Springs, where he can graze and visit with the other creatures to his heart's content. (When farm animals collapse, as Cowvin did, they are called "downed animals." Federal legislation has been introduced, but not passed, to offer them some protection.)

Henrietta, a small, black chicken, was found tied by one leg. The part of her leg below the rope turned black and fell off. This has not deterred this spirited bird, who gets around just fine, moving along somewhat unevenly on both her good leg and her shortened one.

It is true that in this "peaceable kindom" prey and predators do not peacefully coexist, although one encounters many tranquil scenes of animals interacting with one another. One might find a cat perched on top of a pig, enjoying the sun from this porcine vantage point; a dog and turkey might lie next to one another, both enjoying an afternoon nap. A small herd of mixed goats, with their long, velvety ears, cluster together, the shier ones standing back while the more curious goats approach visitors with a direct gaze.

It also is true that some of the residents have their differences. Chester and Brewster, two of the roosters, don't get along too well and need to keep their distance from one another. One turkey, Cranberry, also took a dislike to another turkey, Minerva; they must be kept apart since Minerva has been debeaked and can't defend herself in a squabble. And when I was visiting, and we fed the pigs an afternoon snack of fruit, many of them were definitely not ready to share, emitting shrill squeals and resounding grunts as groups of them dove for the same rolling apple.

Although not a perfect representation of the "peaceable kindom" as envisioned by Isaiah, Poplar Springs Animal Sanctuary comes close in many ways. As I walked around with Terry, meeting the various residents, I felt joy knowing that all of these animals — rescued from dire and dreadful circumstances — were safe. All of the animals were now free to pursue their happiness — whether they were chickens relishing their chance to bathe in the dust; pigs cooling off with a nice, wet, sloppy roll in the mud; or the rooster calling the hens around him to come get the food being offered. The animals now could live the way they were intended to live. So simple, yet so profoundly beautiful and right. The sanctuary protects not just these animals but the integrity of creation. In so doing, it gives a gift to all of us that is beyond measure.

Terry and David's story exemplifies the significance of awareness and compassionate action. Awareness, as I described in the previous chapter, is about love and a loving receptivity toward the whole of creation. No living being is excluded from its encircling arms.

Terry and David's love isn't abstract or distant. It is *fully* realized. Every morning they start their day at 3 or 4 A.M. to tend to each of the animals. The work is hard, dirty, and without time off. In addition to caring for the animals — and taking moments simply to enjoy them — they have to take care of the many administrative details of running a sanctuary. The sanctuary runs solely on private donations. At this point, neither Terry nor David earns a salary from the sanctuary, so David works full-time as a printer. Perhaps one day they will have enough income to pay themselves a stipend and both work reasonable hours caring for the animals. But perhaps not. Despite challenging circumstances, Terry and David are committed to providing a safe haven where animals can live the rest of their lives in peace.

What the animals gain as a result of Terry and David's awareness and compassionate action, manifested as love, is obvious. But Terry and David also benefit from their loving action, which lends meaning to their lives and gives them fulfillment. Loving practice not only benefits the recipients; it also infuses the practitioner with a fullness of being, an immeasurable gift.

Terry and David were not always as aware as they are now. They moved to the land about ten years ago, renting their house when the rest of the farm was a beef cattle ranch. Terry, who had always loved animals, and David made friends with the various cows. They knew their individual personalities and formed relationships with them. One day they heard frightened groaning and mooing from the cattle outside. They watched as the frantic cattle were forced into trucks and driven off to the slaughterhouse.

The sight brought awareness, like a bolt of lightening, to them both simultaneously. Their first action was the decision to stop eating meat, which they had done all their lives, until witnessing their friends being taken to slaughter. This first step of becoming vegetarian evolved into further awareness, and eventually they resolved to open the sanctuary.

Terry and David's actions exemplify the other characteristics of awareness: Awareness requires our attention and action; awareness is not an end in itself but the source of compassion; compassion is necessary to complete awareness; and awareness occurs in a relationship or context.

Before Terry and David were able to expand their awareness they had to pay attention and to care. Feminist theologians, such as Carol Adams and Josephine Donovan, rightly emphasize the significance of care in an ethical response, articulating the necessity of the simple act of paying attention.[6] Terry and David did not ignore the sounds they heard; they did not turn away and occupy themselves with other tasks. They took action by going outside and watching what was happening. They paid attention. This was the first step in their developing awareness.

But they didn't stop at increased awareness; awareness was not an end in itself. Spiritual growth requires a compassionate response to complete, and further, awareness. Not only did they witness the cattle's suffering — they responded to it.

And, finally, Terry and David's awareness and compassion developed in the context of relationships: the relationships they forged with the cattle; the relationship they had with each another; and, eventually, the relationships they formed with other people in the animal sanctuary movement.

In short, they took an important step in their spiritual journey when they acknowledged the cattle's suffering. Following that breakthrough were a series of other steps that kept them on the spiritual path of increased awareness and compassionate action.

Evoking the Possibility of the Peaceable Kindom in Our Lives

Isaiah's vision, as exemplified, although imperfectly, by Poplar Springs, is a powerful image and metaphor. Images and metaphors are not to be taken literally, although carnivores can evolve into vegetarians, as we have seen with Little Tyke. Young reminds us that the Bible is not a scientific text, but rather a source of inspiration and a document of the divine presence in our lives that sets out before us "a hope that contradicts everything we know about life."[7]

No matter what kind of spiritual inclination we possess, or its strength, all of us could benefit from reflecting on the biblical images that present the possibility of a peaceable kindom. Stories such as these beckon us to participate in a higher order of existence, one in which we gain a greater appreciation for the sacredness of life, and one in which we more fully grasp the interdependence of all creation. The image of the peaceable kindom seeks to return us to our own true nature and to a time, as the story goes, when we lived in peace and harmony with one another.

The peaceable kindom is not merely a fanciful, sweet, but unrealistic picture of the world. It is a magnet of hope that can pull us toward a future of compassion, peace, and justice. Some would call that magnet "God." Others might refer to it as "universal activity" or the mystery of nature. Young believes, "We have been called to travel with God on a journey. God is leading us toward a future, where humans and animals coexist in peace, where justice, compassion, and love reign, and where oppression and exploitation are things of the past."[8]

A Buddhist would not discuss God's call, but would refer to karma, the law of causation. It is clear in Buddhist thought that each action we take now, in the present, affects our next action, and subsequent actions. In Hinduism, too, we create who we are step by step, action by action, thought by thought. The cumulative product of all past deeds determines our moral character, and our moral character then influences future actions.[9]

Some may wonder what any one individual can really do to help realize a peaceable kindom. When we look around us, the world seems decidedly unpeaceful. The Tibetan people have been colonized by the Chinese, who intend to subjugate Tibet's ancient culture. Strife and conflict continue in the Middle East; war, starvation, and sickness plague Africa. At home, we witness the plight of the homeless. Our hearts ache at the realization that for many inner-city youth, a meaningless, early death is expected.

Faced with this, we may feel overwhelmed and immobilized. What can we do with our limited time? Perhaps we can send a check, write a letter to our congressperson, join a demonstration, or become active in a local citizen's group. But we can only do so many things; we have to make choices in our lives and sometimes those choices are very difficult.

Our spiritual relationship with animals allows us to practice compassion without having to choose one group over another as we budget the finite time we have in each day. Animals surround and intersect with our lives; they are so integral that we often don't even notice them. Because of the intertwining of human and animal lives, we can act daily to bring into being a peaceable kindom. We can do this by purchasing food, household products, and cosmetics that reject violence. We also can choose clothing made without shedding blood. When we select our entertainment, we can reject those forms that rely on the capture and confinement of animals.

We can do all this without missing a beat in the daily rhythm of our lives. By developing our spiritual relationship with animals, we contribute to a peaceable kindom, and we can do so without having to add any time to our day, or tasks to our agenda. It is that simple, and that profound.

Our relationship with animals, once we become aware of its many dimensions, offers an extraordinary spiritual opportunity. Albert Schweitzer, humanitarian and recipient of the Nobel Peace Price, asserted that reverence for life is much more than the idea of humanism; it is a concept that embraces all living beings. "We must realize that all life is valuable and that we are united to all life," he wrote. "By ethical conduct toward all creatures, we enter into a spiritual relationship with the Universe."[10]

Chapter Four

The New *Kashrut:* The Spiritual Depth of Vegetarianism

I recently spoke with my next-door neighbor and friend Carey about her recent decision, informed by spiritual considerations, to return to a vegetarian diet. Carey is a Christian, but her dedication to turn eating into a spiritual activity may best be described by the term *kashrut* from the Jewish tradition. Kashrut is a system that recognizes that eating — the simple and necessary act in which all of us participate every day — presents us with spiritual possibilities. Kashrut codifies the act of eating, allowing us to recognize those spiritual possibilities and gain a means to participate in holiness.[1]

Jewish texts, which offer considerable support for a vegetarian ideal, speak of eating as essential to holiness; every meal is an opportunity to uplift the world, to participate in *tikkun ha olam* (world repair). Writers on Jewish vegetarianism, such as Roberta Kalechofsky and Richard Schwartz, note that both the traditional kashrut and vegetarianism originate from the same inspiration — a respect for life. They hope to encourage a new kashrut of Jewish vegetarianism.

Closely related to this new kashrut movement is "eco-kashrut," which is advocated in the Jewish renewal movement by the writer and publisher Rabbi Michael Lerner, Rabbi Arthur Waskow, and Rabbi Zalman Schachter-Shalomi.[2] Eco-kashrut expands the precepts of what is kosher beyond food to the larger ecological realm of ethical consumption. Are products grown without the use of earth-destroying pesticides? Are the farmers who raised the crops paid a fair wage? Do the institutions we invest in pollute the environment? In Arthur Waskow's words, the goal of eco-kashrut is one of "protecting the web of life on earth."[3]

Although eco-kashrut expands the realm of ethical questioning, it also focuses specifically on what can be eaten. Michael Lerner notes that "Jewish renewalists are reluctant to eat meat." Waskow concurs with his observation that "larger and larger numbers of contemporary Jews are choosing vegetarianism...."[4] Jews are changing their diets out of respect for animals' pain, and from an awareness that meat and dairy production both contribute to human starvation and harm the environment. Lerner continues, "If you don't eat meat, or milk products...you are automatically kosher. So vegetarian kashrut makes a great deal of sense from a Jewish renewal perspective."[5]

My conversation with Carey puts a human face on the intent of the new kashrut. I know Carey has a keen spiritual inclination, an enthusiastic approach to life, and a strong sense of social justice; she is one of those wonderful spirits who approaches new ideas and people with a truly open mind. I was interested in the particulars of Carey's decision. What spiritual benefits, I wondered, did Carey expect out of her renewed commitment to a vegetarian diet? What were the spiritual implications for her?

First we talked about how her present commitment to vegetarianism differed from an earlier time when she practiced it. Carey reflected that now she finds herself more self-aware and disciplined — more dedicated to following a spiritual path. She also finds it easier to be a vegetarian now than before. Friends and family members have been more tolerant of her decision; a greater variety of vegetarian options are available in restaurants and supermarkets. In general, the world of food is just a bit more hospitable to vegetarians.

Carey's reason for returning to vegetarianism was simple: Her heightened awareness of the "other" — in this case animals used for food — gave her a new respect for all of existence. She could no longer ignore that eating meat requires taking life. Carey has always been attuned to animals and nature. But now, guided by a spiritual realization that all creatures enjoy and desire life, she began to see animals in a new way. This new spiritual awareness allowed her to feel more connected to creation, to overcome the barriers we sometimes place between ourselves and the other.

To put her commitment to vegetarianism into practice, Carey must consciously bring awareness to her eating decisions. In describing the process of her decisions, Carey says that she might find her mouth watering at the aroma of a hamburger on a grill or a turkey roasting in an oven. At first it is an immediate physical response. Then, as she describes it, "my conscience speaks and helps me choose what I want to do in my heart." She explains a process in which her conscience redirects her to think of an image of an animal who suffered and died to create the food her stomach is craving. She looks into her heart for her intent, and from there she makes a choice. "I choose from my best self — my spiritual self," she says. "I choose not to eat meat to honor the value of the creatures whose worth is equal to my own." Carey acknowledges that her decision is not always easy and that she isn't always successful, especially when hurried. But it is always her goal. And it is through this very struggle that Carey develops spiritual insight and strengthens her spiritual resolve.

I was especially struck by one aspect of Carey's commitment — her recognition of her diet as a "heart" exercise, in which she uses her capacity to listen to her deepest feelings rather than submitting to a passing desire. Eating, for her, has become a very thoughtful process, but not an intellectual exercise or a mind game. She relies on her own subjective, heartfelt reactions — the deepest source of her intention.

In other words, Carey senses the divine spark deep within herself, and by recognizing this divinity within, and honoring it by revering life, she falls more deeply into its warming embrace.

Each time Carey decides what to eat she develops her capacity to listen with her heart and to act out of generosity of spirit rather than from narrow, fleeting self-interest. These daily decisions also allow her to transcend her self and connect with others — to act out of a sense of interconnection rather than from an illusion of autonomous individuality. Again, whether one is a Jew or a Christian, a Hindu or a Buddhist, or from any other faith, she or he can participate in the new kashrut by hallowing the eating process. This is exactly what Carey is doing as she continually overrides her potential desire for flesh by examining her heart.

Carey said that if she were relying solely on her will, or responding merely to her knowledge that a vegetarian diet is much more healthy, she might not have been able to sustain her commitment. Carey's understanding of this process as spiritual builds the internal resources she needs to maintain her pledge, action by action, moment by moment.

Carey is not the only one who reaps the benefits. The most obvious beneficiaries, of course, are the animals. Yet many others also profit: in particular, all the people whose lives she touches. Carey's spiritual relationship with animals, realized through her decision to adopt a vegetarian diet, helps her mature into a more compassionate person. When animals help us evolve spiritually, the spiritual results of that growth are manifested in our relationship with them and also in our relationship with the human animals in our lives. What's good for animals is also good for people.

The Origins of the New Kashrut

Carey's intuition that eating is a spiritual activity finds well-documented support in many of the major world religions. One of the best-known exponents of the spirituality of eating is Roberta Kalechofsky. A poet, essayist, novelist, and publisher, she is recognized for her writing on Jewish vegetarianism and the new kashrut. Kalechofsky did not grow up as a vegetarian but became one as her awareness grew of the suffering of animals bred for food. At one time in her life, this doyenne of Jewish vegetarianism was a secretary in a kosher meat cooperative in her hometown of Marblehead, Massachusetts. But her tenure ended when she became exposed to the cruelties of factory farming.

Richard Schwartz, a professor at the City College of New York at Staten Island, submitted a book containing a two-page description of factory-farmed meat to her publishing company. Roberta responded to the material with horror. While the kosher designation required that animals be killed mercifully, she now realized it might not include a requirement to raise the animal humanely. She asked the supervisor of the cooperative how the animals used for their kosher meat were reared; he told her truthfully that all animals farmed for the commercial meat market were raised in the same way — in the confines of a factory farm.

Kalechofsky decided she couldn't eat the meat of tormented animals and quit the kosher meat cooperative, but she had no idea what she and her husband would eat. "I didn't mind eating meat," she says. "I minded eating the meat of tortured animals." She clung to the meat habit because she couldn't imagine Shabbat without chicken. In preparation for the next Shabbat, she called a local farmer on a Thursday and asked him to prepare a chicken for her. The next day, she looked at the chicken as she cooked it — "all brown, with its little legs up, and I felt as if I had ordered its death!" Neither she nor her husband could eat it. They were both "dumbfounded by our feelings."[6] During this period of her life there were other influences on Kalechofsky — reading the novel *The Skin*, by the German-Italian writer Curzio Malaparte, which describes a man finding his lost dog in a research laboratory; discovering Dallas Pratt's book *Alternatives to*

Painful Experiments on Animals in her local library; and adopting the family dog Sasha, who taught her about motherhood, nature, and God. All these events initiated a process of introspection, study, and discovery — a process that resulted in Kalechofsky's prolific and powerful writing on the topic of vegetarianism, vivisection, and other animal-related topics.

In her writing on the Jewish vegetarianism, Kalechofsky traces the origins of the new kashrut to the Hebrew Bible, where we find that Adam and Eve were given only two laws governing what they could eat: "Do not eat from the tree of the knowledge of good and evil," (Gen. 2:14) and "To you I give every herb, seed and green thing. These shall be yours for food." (Gen. 1:30)

Keeping kashrut was simple in the beginning; any plant that came from the earth was naturally kosher. As long as humankind kept vegetarian, they were kosher. Adam and Eve broke the first law of kashrut when they could not resist temptation and tasted the apple; Noah broke the second law after the flood. God, disgusted with the conduct of humankind, immersed the earth in cleansing water after first directing Noah to take his family and two of every type of animal on the ark. After the flood, without orders from God to do so, Noah set up a site where he slaughtered animals for food.

God reluctantly gave Noah permission to eat meat, but as Kalechofsky reminds us, the laws of kashrut "underwent their first complication." Kashrut no longer enjoyed elegant simplicity. God's grudging permission to take the lives of animals came with certain restrictions — no one could eat a limb from a living animal, or consume its blood. Only vegetarian animals were to be used as meat because they were "clean" animals. Animals were to be eaten sparingly, and their lives taken with gratitude and humility, in recognition that their souls belonged to God. Humanity also had to pay a moral price for God's concession: "Humankind would know war and would be separated from the rest of the animal world."[7]

Some scholars contend that God tried to direct the Jewish people back to vegetarianism during their sojourn in the desert, when manna, or bread, became the symbol for God's sustenance. But the people weren't satisfied with manna; they rioted for meat. Kalechofsky observes that Moses made compromises about eating meat in order to preserve his authority. Once again, grudging permission was given to eat meat, as an acknowledgment of human weakness.[8]

Rabbi Abraham Kook, the first chief rabbi of Israel and an esteemed translator of the biblical origins of kashrut for modern times, wrote a pamphlet entitled "A Vision of Vegetarianism and Peace." Recognized as a mystic and a humanitarian, Rabbi Kook argued that the Bible's various injunctions against the selection and preparation of meat were intended to point humans toward a "higher purpose." That higher purpose is a world of universal peace and justice, which would include animals. It is the religious vegetarians, Kook claims, who offer a "spiritual blueprint for tomorrow's world."[9]

Despite the original lapse of Adam and Eve, and the backsliding of their heirs, many instances in both the Bible and Talmud present the vegetarian diet as a spiritual ideal. In addition to the original directive to Adam and Eve to eat a vegetarian diet, the seven sacred foods of biblical Jews were olives, grapes, pomegranates, dates, wheat, barley, and honey (made from dates). Kalechofsky points out that although Judaism has many blessings for food, it has none for meat. In addition, numerous statements in the Talmud discourage meat eating, such as one that flatly warns, "A man should not teach his son to eat meat." As we saw in the preceding chapter, "The Peaceable Kindom," both the messianic and Edenic worlds were pictured as vegetarian. As writer Rabbi Rami M. Shapiro concludes, "Vegetarianism is central to holy living as Judaism has understood it for thousands of years.... Eco-kashrut continues the ancient ideal of eating a vegetarian diet."[10]

In our conversation, Carey sensed this spiritual truth without any historical knowledge of kashrut, or of the present-day movement toward a new kashrut. As we discussed the various images that spring from this renewed tradition, she expressed special appreciation for one, which was the table as an altar. In this representation, the family members who sit at the table are the priests who sanctify the food; the act of eating is an actual manifestation of the holy, an elemental exchange of taking substances from the outer world into our inner being.[11]

The table as altar displays a rich variety of food — it is a feast of love and a celebration of life. The red that appears on this altar is not a symbol of a life given, or taken. It is the deep, shining red of fall apples, the intense purple of beets, and the cheerful hue of a red pepper. The brown on this altar is not that of dead flesh but rather of grains and beans. It is the nut-brown of kamut, the pale tan of basmati rice, and the red-brown of pinto beans — together forming a palette of earthen glory. When we take in the various shapes of the vegetables, fruits, and grains on the table — all sculpted exquisitely by nature — we apprehend that nature is the original artist.

As we participate in the process of eating, we live out the principle of interbeing, or interdependence. What once was "other" becomes part of us. After being taken in, these substances are transformed. What passes through us goes through a continual process of recycling. The nature and quality of the substances we bring into our bodies will directly affect the quality of our inner consciousness. This process has a reverberating effect: Intuitively we sense that we will pay a price if we consume matter that has been polluted with chemicals or obtained through violence. It is hard to imagine that eating tainted substances could help our inner peace or promote spiritual harmony for our planet.

Gandhi noted the significance of eating utensils as symbols, saying that the most violent weapon on earth is the knife used at the dining table. Knives are not needed in a vegetarian meal, which is a violence-free activity. The vegetarian table, if approached with awareness and compassion, becomes a celebration of creation.

Support for the New Kashrut in Other World Religions

Writing from the Christian tradition, Richard Young examines the story in Genesis that describes the seven days of creation. He notes that the sixth day can be divided into three parts: God creates humans in the divine image and gives them "dominion" (1:26–28); God announces a vegetarian diet (1:29–30); and God sees all things are good (1:31)!

Many scholars point out that "dominion" does not mean that humans were given license to use animals any way they see fit. Rather it refers to the responsibility conferred upon humans to be good and wise stewards of animals and the earth. Further, Young points out that humans being given dominion and being created in the divine image are mentioned in the same phrase. This, he contends, is significant. Dominion is a duty, and must be exercised in a way that is congruent with being made in the divine image — out of love, responsibility, and care.[12]

Additionally, Young and other biblical scholars such as Andrew Linzey point out the significance of the order of the passages. The precept giving humans dominion over animals precedes the one that establishes a vegetarian diet. This sequence, they claim, indicates how dominion is to be carried out — without killing or exploiting any creature. As Linzey has commented, "Herb-eating dominion is hardly a license for despotism." He also notes that the authors of this passage were not vegetarians, so that in order to espouse a vegetarian diet they had to rely on their moral intuition rather than their own dietary practices. They were convinced that violence between humans and animals was not part of God's original plan for creation. Linzey contends that the fact that they were meat-eaters themselves underscores the radical message of these passages, that is, they had no vegetarian "ax to grind."[13]

For many Christians the most symbolic and spiritually meaningful meal is the Eucharist. It is their central ritual, manifesting the most profound and sweeping vision of what life under God's grace can be. Stephen Webb poses the question, "What kind of nourishment does it offer?" To find out, he examines the "theological logic" of the meal, suggesting that its importance lies in the fact that the bread and wine of the Eucharist are, both literally and symbolically, a vegetarian meal. In the Eucharist, suffering is commemorated but no pain is inflicted and no death is necessary. The central themes of death, resurrection, and transformation resonate in this vegetarian meal.[14]

Webb concludes that the phrase "Take this and eat," which is uttered by the Eucharist officiate to the celebrant, is not only an invitation but a caution. The caution, as expressed in words that Jesus might have used: "Do not eat what can feel the same pain that I feel. As you eat your memories of me, eat life and peace, not violence and death."[15]

Like Roberta Kalechofsky, who asserts that there is a new kashrut of vegetarianism developing in Judaism, Webb suggests that a "future is breaking" in Christianity's communion meal. In this coming time, we will recognize that animals fall within the embrace of God's grace and redemption. By partaking in the vegetarian Eucharist, spiritual seekers give voice to the call to build a world of harmony and justice. After all, "what we eat is what we believe."[16]

I know people who believe differently. In a former neighborhood of mine, I was acquainted with a combined family of five in which three different faiths were represented — Buddhist, Christian, and one individual's eclectic blend of spiritual traditions. For spiritual reasons, however, all members of the family have adopted a vegetarian diet. So while they may not be able to worship in exactly the same way in other instances, they do share their beliefs when they gather together to eat. All are dedicated to nonviolence and social justice, volunteering their time and money to various groups serving those goals. And when they gather around the dining room table, they find spiritual renewal together in their commitment to nonviolence by sharing a vegetarian meal.

Anyone who has ever had the good fortune to eat at an Asian

restaurant specializing in vegetarian cuisine has experienced first-hand the incorporation of spiritual awareness into food preparation. Many "mock" meat dishes are made out of soy and gluten rather than animal flesh. Buddhist monks responsible for feeding other monks in the monastery were the clever chefs who invented these tasty, interesting, and healthy dishes. Their inspiration came from the Buddhist principle of *ahimsa*, which emphasizes compassion and a reverence for all life. D. T. Suzuki, Zen monk and author, points out that compassion is the foundation of Buddhism. And the *Mahaparinirvana Sutra* states that "the eating of meat extinguishes the seed of great compassion."[17] The monks' efforts enabled others to develop the "seed of great compassion" by making eating a spiritual activity, one that reveres life and also eschews violence.

Buddhists, especially those of the *Mahayana* school, can refer to numerous references in their religious texts that support Buddhism's vegetarian ideal. Philip Kapleau, a Zen roshi who has written a number of significant books on Buddhism, documents the Buddhist case for vegetarianism. Basing his argument on the first precept of Buddhism, which espouses harmlessness to living beings, or ahimsa, he carefully examines the texts of Buddhism's Mahayana and Theravada traditions. He systematically discusses the conflict between the Mahayana texts, which clearly condemn eating meat, and some passages of the Theravada texts, which condone it by claiming that the Buddha ate meat. Kapleau contends that on this topic the Mahayana texts preserve the authentic intention of Buddhism. Why then are there references to meat eating in the Theravada texts of the Pali canon? Simple, says Kapleau. Monks attached to consuming meat put them there. He notes that the Buddhist canon, like all of the world's religious literature, developed gradually over time. As it evolved, various individuals, with varying tastes, opinions, and interpretations, changed it along the way.

Ultimately, Kapleau says, determining exactly what the Buddha would say about any topic is beyond our historical reach. This is why

Zen emphasizes that truth is grasped directly, and not derived from intellectual formulas. Avoiding violence in our eating cannot rest on what the Buddha said or didn't say, but rather on something more immediate: "…on innate moral goodness, compassion, and pity, which, when liberated, lead us to value all forms of life."[18]

Other Asian religions, also under the influence of ahimsa, expound a vegetarian diet for spiritual reasons. Ahimsa, or harmlessness to all living beings — which would certainly exclude eating them — pervades Indian religious consciousness and religious history. Ahimsa itself comes from India's Jain tradition, as we will see in the next chapter. Strictures against meat eating can be found in the *Vedas* and *Upanishads*, sacred Sanskrit texts, that preceded the Buddha. To this day, meat eating is frowned upon by most believing Hindus. Southern Indian cooking, another delightful cuisine, is typically vegetarian, reflecting the spiritual influence of Indian religious teaching.

The Spiritual Benefits of the New Kashrut

Rabbi Michael Kramer recounts how he became a vegetarian because of his daughter Rachel. When she was ten years old he ordered duck for her at a Chinese restaurant. She took one look at it and refused to eat it, saying she wouldn't eat anything that reminded her of Donald Duck. This was the beginning of Rachel's vegetarianism; her father and mother followed her example several years later. About spiritual maturation, Rabbi Kramer writes, "We are never there, but always reaching." Far from achieving some spiritual perfection, he still asserts that vegetarianism demonstrates a higher regard for life than eating meat. For him, it is an affirmation that "in at least one area of my life I am following a path of righteousness."[19] Adopting a vegetarian diet — and opening himself to his daughter's sensitivity — offered Rabbi Kramer a way to feel he was spiritually on track.

The new kashrut not only benefits one's spiritual welfare, but also enhances one's physical well-being. Meat and dairy products contribute to a host of diseases — heart disease, high blood pressure, diabetes, atherosclerosis, cancer, and osteoporosis. (Osteoporosis, contrary to conventional wisdom, is associated with high protein intakes, not insufficient calcium. Even with high calcium intake, the more excess protein in the diet, the greater the loss of calcium from the bones.) Animal products simply are not essential for our health. The American Dietetic Association took the position that vegetarian meals are "healthful,... nutritionally adequate, and provide health benefits in the prevention and treatment of certain diseases."[20]

The costs of a meat- and dairy-based diet are high. One estimate is that the annual health care cost of eating meat is $50 billion — the same amount spent each year to treat the effects of smoking. Being overweight can also contribute to a variety of health problems, and there is a correlation between being overweight and consuming a flesh-based diet. Vegetarians weigh about twenty pounds less than meat eaters in this country.

A plant-based diet is not just good for you because of what you don't eat; vegetables have clear positive effects on human health. Research has shown, for example, that cruciferous vegetables, such as broccoli and cauliflower, play a part in preventing cancer. The isoflavones found in soy products may reduce our risk of cancer, lower our cholesterol, and assist in the absorption of calcium; onions and garlic protect against viruses, cancer, and high blood pressure; and fiber lowers serum cholesterol. The health benefits of a plant-based diet are many, and growing. As Howard Lyman, ex-cattle rancher turned vegetarian activist, remarks, "You never switch on the news to learn that a medical study at Harvard has revealed that roast beef boosts the immune system, or that fried chicken helps prevent arthritis, or that ham is good for the prostate."[21] And you never will. Meat and dairy products simply do not promote human health.

Acting from thoughtful spiritual and ethical considerations, individuals who practice the new kashrut not only feel better about themselves, they also protect the environment. The rainforest is destroyed, in large measure, to make way for cattle grazing. By saving these and other forests from destruction, the habitats for all types of free-roaming animals are also saved. In turn, ecological balances are preserved and more free-roaming animals such as lions, bears, coyotes, foxes, and bobcats are saved from being shot or poisoned by ranchers. The new kashrut will also help end the ecologically irresponsible practice of growing grain to feed cattle rather than people. (Eighty percent of grains and legumes grown in the U.S. are fed to livestock. And even as experts agree that the rivers and oceans are being depleted of fish, one-third of all fish caught are fed to livestock.)

With the new kashrut, there will be less cattle waste, which emits nitrates and bacteria into groundwater, thus poisoning surrounding streams, rivers, and aquifers. The land devoted in developing countries to growing grain for cattle, or to cattle grazing, can be used to produce food for their own hungry people.

Most experts agree that world hunger can be solved only by the adoption of a vegetarian diet. The reasons are obvious. It takes sixteen pounds of grain to create one pound of beef. The same amount of grain could feed thirty-two people. Cattle are fed, yet people are going hungry. The Council on Agricultural Science and Technology calculated that the currently available land could feed ten billion people with new techniques — if the world population became vegetarian. But if they don't, human starvation will continue.[22]

It isn't often that something is so clear. There are no downsides to the new kashrut. It is good for the individual, both spiritually and physically. It is good for human health. It is good for the environment and it addresses the important social justice issue of world hunger. To my thinking, the case is compelling.

Chapter Five

Ahimsa: Cultivating Nonviolence toward Animals

A*himsa* — harmlessness to all living things — was first born in India, and flowered in the East. Theology professor Christopher Key Chapple, who traced the origins of this doctrine of nonviolence in his book *Nonviolence to Animals, Earth, and Self in Asian Traditions,* notes that modern scholarship has not determined exactly how and where ahimsa began. Based on his research, Chapple believes that some form of religion that included the practice of meditation and the veneration of animals existed in Indus Valley cities as early as 3000 B.C. While it is not possible to establish that ahimsa was practiced in this early civilization as it is today, there is evidence of an "iconographic and thematic continuity" that links the early Indus civilization to classical and modern Jainism. Of all religions, Jainism embraced the principle of harmlessness most, believing that "all beings are fond of life; they like pleasure and hate pain, shun destruction and like to live, and they long to live. To all, life is dear."[1]

Jainism, which was founded by Mahavira, a contemporary of the Buddha, has been called the "conscience of India." One of the many acts of charity the Jainas perform is to establish and administer animal hospitals. Motivated by their desire to harm other beings as little as possible, the Jainas developed a systematic analysis of life forms, organized into five categories and based on the number of senses a life form enjoys. Five-sense creatures include humans and other mammals such as monkeys, cattle, and horses, and also parrots, fish, birds, and octopuses. Insects can have either four or three senses. Those with four senses are the larger insects such as bees, flies, and grasshoppers. Insects such as moths, ants, and mosquitoes are thought to lack a sense of taste and touch, and therefore comprise the three-sensed life forms. Mollusks, crustaceans, worms, and leeches, are thought to possess only two senses, those of taste and touch. One sense entities include trees, plants, water bodies, fire bodies, and wind bodies. Finally, there are rocks and minerals, which are considered inanimate, but which may house microscopic beings. Jainas, who are strict vegetarians, eat as far down the sense hierarchy as possible, consuming only one-sensed creatures. In this way they reduce the injury they cause to other living beings as much as possible.

While ahimsa may be most fully expressed in the Jain religion, it also occupies a significant place in Hinduism. Undoubtedly Hinduism adopted the doctrine of ahimsa through the influence of the Jain religion. At the same time, Steven Rosen, another scholar of religion, notes that references to ahimsa are found throughout the Hindu Vedas.[2] For Hinduism's classical yoga system, ahimsa forms the basis for all ethical action. It is the cornerstone of the "yamas," the specific ethical principles that make up the first limb of the eight-limbed Raja yoga system of Patanjali, author of the *Yoga Sutras*.[3] Judith Lasater writes about yoga philosophy, "It is often said that if one can perfect the practice of ahimsa, one need learn no other practice of yoga, for all the other practices are subsumed in it."[4] She suggests that all the practices after the first limb — for example, breathing and postures — cannot be accomplished without ahimsa.

Also central to Buddhism, ahimsa provides the basis for its first precept. In discussing the rationale for the principle of harmlessness, Roshi Philip Kapleau explains that all existences are unified and harmonized and all existences seek to maintain this unity. Willfully taking life creates disharmony and disunity; it also blunts those feelings of compassion that arise from our Buddha-mind. Exhortations to practice ahimsa can be found in various Buddhist texts. In the *Dhammapada*, for example, the Buddha is quoted as saying, "A man is not noble if he injures living creatures; because a man has pity on all living creatures, therefore is a man called noble. The true Ariya (nobleman) practices Ahimsa...compassion, nonviolence."[5] In addition, respect for life, and for animals specifically, can be found in the numerous references to animals in the teachings of both the Buddha and later Buddhists. These texts give examples of animals acting commendably, and sometimes even earning rebirth in human form as a reward. Animals are also depicted as capable of hearing and learning the teachings of the Buddha. Kapleau even raises the possibility of giving the precepts to an animal. I don't know exactly how that would work, but it is a tempting possibility to consider for one's animal companions.[6]

Deer As Teachers of Ahimsa

The principle of ahimsa came alive to me recently when I became involved in a grassroots movement to stop the proposed slaughter of a small herd of fifteen to twenty deer who were entering Brookside Gardens, a fifty-acre display garden operated by the Maryland-National Capital Park and Planning Commission in Montgomery County, Maryland. Brookside shares a boundary with Wheaton Regional Park, where a growing population of deer live. Deer do not read maps and often leave the confines of the regional park to forage in the adjacent Brookside Gardens and residential backyards. According to park officials, the deer, tempted by their favorite foods — azalea bushes and tulips, among other delectable flora — were entering Brookside and feasting on prized horticultural collections. Evidently, the deer's foraging damaged various displays at Brookside

— the extent of the damage varied depending on who was making the assessment.

Over the course of a few years, the Brookside park officials tried various methods to keep the deer out. They placed repellents and netting around certain plants to dissuade them from eating the foliage and surrounded the gardens with a ten-foot fence. They also installed a cattle guard at one of the gates. But none of these methods worked well enough. After three years of trying to no avail, park officials concluded that the only solution was to slaughter the deer, and made arrangements to bring in sharpshooters to kill them.

I attended a public meeting at a local high school, well-attended by county residents, at which park officials presented the reasoning behind their decision. After the presentation, members of the audience were permitted two minutes apiece to comment or ask questions. For two hours, scores of individuals, some supporting the plan but more opposed to it, went to the microphones to make their statements.

As one could imagine, debating whether or not it was necessary or ethical to slaughter the offending deer evoked considerable passion on both sides of the question. I sympathized with both the park officials and the citizens who were dismayed by the damage the deer had done. At the same time, in my hierarchy of values, if forced to choose, the lives of deer would take precedence over the lives of tulips. That is not to say I do not value tulips and other plants. Rather, while both plants and animals are living forms, they do not possess the same capacity to enjoy life. Plants do not experience pleasure or pain; they do not exhibit individual personalities; they do not have their own desires and interests. Deer do. The destruction of a tulip and of a deer cannot be equated at any level of analysis — biologically, ethically, or spiritually.

The fact that the deer, having become accustomed to people, were semi-domesticated made the idea of their slaughter even more gruesome. Thinking no harm would come to them, the herd might allow the sharpshooters to get quite close before killing them.

After hearing the park officials' presentations and various citizen comments, it became clear to me and many others that a choice did not have to be made between deer and tulips. Other solutions were available.

The park officials had failed to consider some obvious alternatives. The deer were getting in through open gates. Converting the eight pedestrian gates to turnstiles would keep the deer out, as would double-gating the two large, roadside gates through which cars (and sometimes deer) entered. Posting staff during the peak hours of deer foraging at the two large roadside gates, which were clearly the major point of entry for the herd, would also keep the unwanted animals out. While it is true that each of these remedies would require some expenditure of park funds, they would be minor compared with the investment the park had already made.

The sharpshooting program they proposed also had a cost, and would not permanently solve the problem. Other herds would eventually make their way through the gates and then *that* group would have to be killed, and then the next and the next. Instead of a grand display of nature's beauty, an oasis in the midst of a dense metropolitan area, Brookside Gardens would become a killing field. Yet another suggested solution — less than ideal because of the trauma to the deer — was to relocate them; one participant offered his multi-acre property as a home for the herd, and another agreed to underwrite their transportation.

Many of the people who spoke at the meeting did not agree with those intent on protecting the lives of the deer. Some were quite distressed by the damage to the plants and wanted the deer eliminated. One woman who spoke in favor of the park officials' deer removal plan recounted how her mother's visit from California to see the famous tulips at Brookside Gardens was spoiled because of the damage done by the deer. A man complained that those of us who wished to protect the deer were elevating animals to the status of humans, and even making them "superior to humans."

I'm sure that some of the supporters of the plan assumed the sharpshooter strategy was humane, and that the deer would not suffer. More likely, though, the other deer would become frantic and race away in fear after the first was shot. With adrenaline surging through their bodies, they would crash through whatever was in their way to try to escape — brick walls, bushes, gates. Some would injure themselves as they fled. It would take not minutes, but hours, and probably days, to pursue and finally exterminate the last deer. Throughout this time the deer, filled with intense fear and panic, would suffer greatly.

As I sat in the midst of this heated debate, I had my own personal and public reactions to the comments I heard. I tried my best to step back from the immediacy of what was being said to think about ahimsa, and how the exacting lessons of this doctrine of harmlessness might be applied to this situation. Although ahimsa has a simple definition — harmlessness to all living beings — it is actually a complex concept with many implications. First of all, the nonviolence advocated by ahimsa does not refer simply to not harming another physically.

The practice of harmlessness asks that we scrutinize not just our actions but also our inner thoughts and feelings. Gandhi reminded us that ahimsa covers subtle as well as overt acts of violence. Just as important to the practice of this principle is freeing ourselves of violence in thought, feeling, and word. Lying, anger, hatred, resentment, envy, and egoism — all of these behaviors violate the spirit of ahimsa.[7] Practicing ahimsa, then, would include not only the action of not killing the deer but also that, as one advocated for the deer, one's own inner thoughts and feelings should be free of violence. This does not mean that a person will never experience anger, hatred, or envy. Rather it means that one should not harbor those feelings, or act on them. As a psychologist, I am well aware that emotions are important sources of information for us. Our goal should be to notice what we feel, contemplate what the feeling is telling us, and then decide how we will use the feeling to take action or make a decision.

In addition to this expanded notion of harmlessness, which includes thoughts and feelings as well as actions, we turn next to three other important features of ahimsa: its emphasis on the continuity of existence, its association with karma, and the invitation to love one's enemy. We can again extract their lessons by applying them to the situation with the deer at Brookside Garden.

Continuity of Existence

The reality of interdependence and seamless unity forms the basis for nonviolence. At the deepest level of our being, our true nature is being open to life, to consciousness, and to the inconceivable, transcendental reality that encompasses us, the deer, and the rest of nature belong.[8] At this transcendental level of reality, no boundaries exist between us and the deer — or between any one of us and any others. All life is part of an ocean of consciousness. Individual waves take shape and disappear, only to reappear again in the mist of this vast ocean. While the individual waves appear to have a distinct shape and form, this is illusory; they are simply a manifestation of the all-encompassing, abiding ocean of consciousness. So it is with us. While we think we have a distinct shape and form — an "I-ness" — at the most profound plane of existence we are consciousness, without name or form.

We are linked together in a world of reciprocal dependence, one in which other persons, animals, and elements coexist. Instead of organizing the natural world into discrete categories, the concept of ahimsa constructs a world characterized by a dynamic flow of interaction and interconnection. In his classic book on the basic philosophy of Buddhism, Walpola Rahula explains, "I am only relatively not you and you are only relatively not me."[9]

We can distinguish an absolute reality of oneness from the practical, everyday reality in which we live. In this practical reality, we are trained to notice differences. An important aspect of a child's cognitive maturation depends on making distinctions between categories and then organizing those categories into ever more complex networks and systems. At this practical level, the categories we use to organize differences are useful and necessary. At a spiritual level, however, the tendency to organize the world this way can be a hindrance. While we may be accustomed to focusing on the differences between us and deer and other animals, these distinctions, at an underlying level of reality, are illusions. If we only take into account that which separates and distinguishes us from one another, we miss the possibility of experiencing the transcendental reality that surrounds our being. The practitioner devotes herself to trying to enact ahimsa in the practical reality in which we live — that is, to catch glimpses of the absolute reality in the midst of our everyday lives.

Those who spoke in favor of the slaughter saw the deer as nuisances and pests, as "things" that needed to be disposed of. Often they spoke of the deer with great vehemence and animosity. Perhaps some had become desensitized to violence, which blunted their ability to respond to the deer with empathy. All of us are vulnerable to this kind of deadening of our senses. By practicing ahimsa we train ourselves to open to the perspectives and situations of others; ahimsa is our best antidote for lapsing into insensitivity.

The yawning, unbridgeable gap was obvious — they saw little or no connection between themselves and the deer. Listening to their comments, I was reminded of Chapple's observation: "When other stands opposed to self, violence can proceed. When other is seen as self, nonviolence can prevail."[10] They were able to sanction violence as a solution to the "deer problem" because they viewed the deer as opposed to, and other than, themselves. It was only their perceived separateness from the deer that permitted them to accept such a plan.

I didn't know any of the plan's proponents individually. I assume that, like most of us, they are trying to lead good, ethical lives. In this instance, however, I believe that they have been misdirected by their view of the deer as "other." As "other," the deer could be eradicated with no consequence. I do not mean to imply that these people lack some spiritual quality that the protectors of the deer possess. First, it is not my intention to judge people on some kind of "ahimsa scale"; to do so would definitely violate the spirit of ahimsa! I use these illustrations to show that nonviolence is not an abstract concept, but an attitude and behavior that can be incorporated into every aspect of our lives. Second, even those who took a position of nonviolence toward the deer didn't always show that same attitude toward their opponents on this issue. Feeling they were fighting against great odds, some of the friends of the deer screamed at their detractors, shaking with fury at those who would harm the defenseless animals.

Paradoxically, the principle of ahimsa teaches us to refrain from using our power against others, and yet the concept itself, because of its moral strength and integrity, has enormous power to influence others. Although ahimsa is put in the negative — that is, do not harm or injure — it is the most positive of principles. It is a powerful moral and psychological force that has moved nations and shaped history, as illustrated in the movements led by Gandhi and Martin Luther King, Jr.

Ahimsa is as exacting a doctrine as it is powerful. It requires us to remember that we are not different from the person who opposes us — even when that person wants to slaughter deer and says so with great fury. As I sat in my seat at the public meeting and heard various speakers rail against the deer, I felt surges of anger, contempt, and violence within myself. At those moments I saw the individuals who spoke against these defenseless creatures as the enemy and as different, and other, than me. I could feel the distance between us: It was hard, unyielding, and dead. Realizing what I was doing, I tried to remove myself from my emotion and listen to what they were saying — not agreeing with them, but respecting the sincerity of their feelings and beliefs. This was not easy to do. But nobody ever said that practicing nonviolence would be easy.

The Jaina tradition offered me a framework for listening to the views of others with whom I passionately disagree, like the proponents of the Brookside deer kill. According to the Jaina perspective, one avoids two extremes: rigid positions that make one offensive, or ambivalent positions with no sense of right and wrong. Both violate the spirit of ahimsa. Avoiding both the nihilism of unconditional relativism and the rigidity of an unyielding absolutism, the Jaina tradition proposes approaching others' ideas with tolerance, while maintaining one's certainty in, and commitment to, the Jaina ethical and philosophical system.

At the intellectual level, the ahimsa doctrine of "respect for life" becomes "respect for the opinion of others." As Chapple asks, how can a particular point of view — even one that supports killing deer — be derided if the holder of that opinion is no different from oneself?[11] We cannot claim to be at one with the deer but separate from their killers. Respect for another person's opinion does not mean, however, that one must forfeit one's own point of view. And it does not mean that one has to be tepid or meek in one's position.

A story from the Vedas illustrates this caveat: A wandering monk encounters a large, threatening snake who has been menacing a village. Seeing this, the monk teaches the snake about ahimsa; the snake takes the teachings to heart and changes his ways. When the monk next visits the village a year later, however, he sees that this once magnificent snake is now skinny and covered with bruises. The pacified snake has been harassed by schoolchildren who throw rocks at him; afraid of this onslaught, he rarely leaves his hiding place to hunt. The monk shakes his head at the snake, saying, "I did advise against violence, but I never told you not to hiss."[12]

If we rely on a philosophical and ethical foundation that proposes a unity and continuity to existence and promotes a respect for all life, then we must listen to those with whom we disagree respectfully and attentively. We can confront them vigorously, present our views with conviction, and work assiduously to defeat them. However, if in the process we hate them, or use violent words or thoughts against them, we lose the argument, since we both violate a respect for life and ignore the unity of existence. Conversely, by attending to the opinions of those with whom we disagree, we honor and strengthen the very principles we espouse. We must not forget that we are united in existence with the deer killer as well as with the deer.

The Link to Karma

With its emphasis on the continuity of existence, not just among existing life forms but all life, past, present, and future, ahimsa is naturally linked with the idea of karma. Karma, which follows the law of cause and effect, "is a manifestation of the moral consequences deriving from the totality of an individual's self-expression in life."[13] An individual's karma — her moral history — determines the state and quality of the life form in which she will be reincarnated. In other words, what goes around comes round.

Roshi Philip Kapleau illustrates this point with an anecdote from Buddhism's Jakata tales, in which a Brahmin is about to sacrifice a goat. After he turns the goat over to his assistants for preparation, the animal bursts into peals of laughter, followed by great weeping. The Brahmin asks the goat why he is acting this way. The goat answers that in his previous existence he himself was a Brahmin. And, like the Brahmin who is about to kill him to honor an ancestor, he had also sacrificed a goat in just the same way. As a result of this killing, he is doomed to be reborn as a goat for his next 500 existences; in each one he is to have his head cut off. The animal then explains that he laughed with joy knowing that would be his 500th existence and end of his punishment. And he wept because of the 500 existences of sorrow the Brahmin would bring upon himself for severing his head.[14]

Such stories capture the essence of the teaching in a way that discursive explanations cannot — as does the Jaina concept of karma as a physical entity, a "viscous mass," that attaches itself to the life force, causing attachment and its consequence, suffering. Chapple offers the following illustration, which depicts a continuum from violence to nonviolence, and the type of karma each produces:

A person desiring a mango might uproot and kill an entire tree in order to obtain the fruit, an act of violence that would produce black karma. Another person might chop the tree down to achieve his goal of a few mangoes. For this he would earn blue karma, which is slightly less intense, but still dark. Someone who spared the trunk of the tree but cut off a number of limbs for his mangoes would earn less severe karma. Yet another person, who more carefully, and less violently, lopped off a number of branches to reach the mangoes, would achieve a brighter, orange-red karma. Finally, the individual who waits for a mango to drop to the ground before he eats it would earn white karma.[15]

I don't know what color karma the proposed plan to slaughter the deer would have produced, perhaps blue or gray. We don't know why the park officials failed to explore all possible solutions before they devised the plan of slaughtering the deer, or why they stopped short of adapting the entrances to successfully deter the deer. They did take several measures, presumably in good faith. Their failure to solve the problem humanely would have been more egregious if they had not even examined other options, and simply proposed slaughter as the first solution. Although I was appalled by the plan, I also know it could have been much worse. They could have opened the gardens to bow hunters, allowing children as young as twelve to kill the deer, which has been done in some hunts. Over half the deer killed by bow and arrow suffer a slow, agonizing death. Often they wander off to die hours or days later. This would have inflicted even greater trauma on the deer, producing the blackest karma for all involved.

Whether or not one accepts the notion that karma affects one's future lives — a concept that first requires accepting the idea of reincarnation — as a psychologist, I am well aware that we may "transmigrate" between different realms of existence every day. Psychologically, we can place ourselves in the realm of the "hungry ghost," where we feel starved for attention and recognition; we might then return to the realm of human existence, presumably with more capacity for awareness; then perhaps we might slip into the animal realm, where we lose our capacity for reflection. On any one day we may move between these different realms of existence any number of times.

I am also aware that all of us produce karma for ourselves in *this* lifetime. The actions an individual takes establish a pattern that then guides their actions. If I am habitually suspicious of new ideas and people, I will grow more suspicious as I age. If, however, realizing I am unnecessarily suspicious, I actively seek to overcome this limitation, I can produce new patterns of response and redirect my reactions to new ideas and people. If I am successful, as I engage in a new pattern of response, I will open myself to new, enriching possibilities. Perhaps we do pass from this life on to others; perhaps we don't. It makes no difference. We can be certain that we are responsible for whatever karma we generate this time around, which is in itself enough to think about.

The Brookside Gardens conflict remains unresolved. After the plan to kill the deer was met with vigorous opposition, park officials acceded to let the animal rights organizations present alternative plans. They also agreed to have a landscape architect review ways in which the gates might be made secure. The deer herd in question remains in jeopardy, however. Park officials remain adamant that they must be removed, despite discussions about better gating. And some county residents have stated that they don't want the deer moved to their area. Meanwhile animal activists, with the cooperation of friendly garden neighbors, are placing corn and apples outside the park gates, hoping to lure the deer out and keep them out.

How this conflict is resolved will produce its own karma. If park officials and animal activists can arrive at a successful resolution and the deer are kept away from the plants without violence, this will reinforce for these park officials, as well as for others who find themselves in similar situations, that peaceful solutions are possible. If negotiations break down and the deer are killed, this will only reinforce the idea that violence is a viable solution to conflicts.

Loving Your Enemy

As we have seen, the principle of ahimsa sets a high standard. A doctrine of nonviolence includes not only actions, but also thoughts, feelings, and words. Ahimsa also requires us to remember that existence is continuous, and as a consequence, we are, in this case, at one with not only the deer but also the deer killers. Because existence is continuous, with each life interrelated and interchangeable, the quality of ahimsa in our lives has direct bearing on our spiritual character. Yet another requirement of ahimsa is that we love our enemy.

Mahatma Gandhi and Martin Luther King, Jr., made perhaps the most eloquent pleas to love our enemies. Nonviolence formed the basis for these two extraordinary men's philosophies. They embodied the ideal of spirituality strengthened by ethics and the commitment to social justice, thus changing the course of their nation's histories and inspiring other leaders of social justice movements to follow their example. When Gandhi and King asked their supporters to love the very people they were battling, they were not referring to the love we usually think of. They were asking us to learn to love in a particular way — without personal needs or attachment, rather than solely from personal investment in another. Often when we think of love, we think of our immediate loved ones. This kind of love, of course, is important. The love of ahimsa, however, takes us to another level. Ahimsa conveys a universal love, which Gandhi called "pure love" — a love for the broad sweep of creation, as well as for the particular beings in one's life.

Martin Luther King, Jr.'s commitment to nonviolence was influenced not only by Gandhi but also by his Christian faith. In the simplest terms, he believed that violence is derived from hate and that hate contradicts God. How, King asked, can we join God in creating a just community if we use violence? King's commitment to nonviolence was tested many times. One dramatic example occurred when his home was bombed with his wife and infant child inside. At the time of the bombing, King was leading a meeting of his supporters. After being told of the assault, and after determining that his wife and child were safe, he turned his attention to the people at the meeting. He urged them not to panic or retaliate in any way but rather to maintain their philosophy of nonviolence. Then he rushed home to see his family. When he arrived he found hundreds of people, angry and shocked by this horrific crime, gathered in front of his house. His instructions to this restless group were the same ones he had given earlier — he urged them not to seek revenge. Setting a perfect example of ahimsa, King implored them "to confront the problem with love."[16]

Gandhi and King knew, of course, that the injunction to love your enemy was the most difficult of goals. Both men acknowledged that they wrestled with the standard themselves. Yet these two spiritual leaders also believed that loving one's enemy did not weaken oneself; rather it provided one with the most potent implements with which to advance a cause. King believed in the creative, redemptive power of love — that in loving one's enemy one has the power to transform him. He claimed that, in the long run, nonviolence disarmed the oppressor, weakened his morale, exposed his defenses, and worked on his conscience.

Both men based their lives and the leadership of two historic movements on the belief that nonviolence was a sign not of weakness but of strength, that only a strong and courageous person could achieve nonviolence. In fact, Gandhi advised that if given a choice only between cowardice and violence, he would sanction violence. He did not think that the nonviolence of a person who felt helpless was meaningful. But Gandhi did not see himself, or India, as helpless.[17]

Their strength flowed from moral and spiritual forces; their weapons were love and passive resistance. Their faith was strengthened, in the face of terrible violence, by their dedication to their ideals and the discipline they practiced.

I certainly haven't achieved the goal of loving those who would kill the deer at Brookside Gardens. I know, however, how important it is to my spiritual health to try. In striving to come closer to this ideal, I not only support my own spiritual development, I also better serve the animals I seek to protect.

Examples of Ahimsa

Swami Prabhavananda and the writer Christopher Isherwood, in their commentary on the yoga aphorisms of Patanjali, observed that when an individual truly renounces violence in all of its manifestations — direct action, internal feelings, and speech — one senses a particular atmosphere of peace around that person.[18] All of us are sensitive to such an atmosphere, including animals. Prabhavananda and Isherwood note that free-roaming animals, who otherwise might fear human contact, are relaxed in the presence of a truly peaceful person. They refer to one woman who handled deadly snakes without incident; she explained that the reptiles knew she would never hurt them.

Most of us have met someone who emanates such calm. Such people can have a profound effect on those around them. Shohaku Okumuru, a Zen priest, was our houseguest while leading a retreat in our area. My dog Toshi, while usually quite affectionate and sociable, is sometimes suspicious and aloof to newcomers.

When Shohaku entered our home, instead of rushing up, barking, and warily sniffing him, Toshi was relaxed and friendly. As my husband, Sam, Shohaku, and I talked, Toshi stayed close to Shohaku, even settling down to lay at his feet. Later when Shohaku sat on his futon bed to look at his notes, Toshi — who weighs over 100 pounds —

tried to crawl into his lap! Shohaku emits a tranquility — a feeling of ahimsa — to which Toshi responded.

I don't think it is just human animals that manifest ahimsa. I have also known dogs who gave off an aura of peacefulness. While visiting dog parks I have noticed that invariably one or two dogs will remain above the minor squabbles and challenges of the other dogs. It isn't because these dogs are docile; some are quite lively and playful — even mischievous. But they possess an internal balance that other dogs sense and respond to.

The animal-releasing ceremonies of Buddhism provide another vivid example of ahimsa in action. The origins of these ceremonies come from Buddhist scriptures, which encourage the rescue of non-human animals. The great Buddhist leader Ashoka, an Indian emperor from 265 to 238 B.C., followed the injunction to liberate and protect all living beings. He issued a "Pillar Edict" making it illegal to kill certain animals and exhorting his followers from injuring or killing *any* living being. Japanese emperors in ancient times also issued decrees liberating animals, as did those in China.

In fact, until the Chinese Communist revolution in 1949, the practice of releasing animals was common. Many large monasteries in China would keep a pool of water for released creatures near their main gate. The pious would drop live fish they had rescued from fishmongers into this pool. Cows, pigs, and other land animals were rescued and sheltered in stables behind the monastery. At times, thousands of animals were liberated en masse as offerings to the Bodhisattva of Compassion, *Kuan-yin*.[19]

The Buddhist release ceremonies are still practiced today. Roshi Philip Kapleau introduced this practice to the Rochester Zen Center, where he resides. Other groups also have adopted this custom, such as a Buddhist sangha, or community, in Vancouver, whose members, on the last Sunday of every month, visit the market in Chinatown, carrying a large bucket. Walking through the aisles of the market, they select sea creatures who seem healthy enough to survive release.

By the end of their mission, they have collected clams, angel fish, gold-fish, lobsters, and crabs. Before their release, the sea animals travel to the Buddhist temple, where a short ceremony is performed. The Great Compassion mantra is recited and they are blessed. Then they are dri-ven to a nearby inlet where they gain their freedom.[20]

Putting Ahimsa into Practice

Practicing ahimsa in our daily lives is simultaneously simple and exceedingly hard. The concept of ahimsa is uncomplicated, clear, and unmistakable: Do no violence in thought, word, or deed. One imme-diately recognizes the righteousness of this injunction. Other reli-gious concepts, such as the Holy Trinity, or the Buddhist concept of emptiness, may invite scholarly debate and exegesis. Ahimsa's mean-ing is apparent and its validity indisputable. Who could argue against reverence for life?

In the desire to perfect the practice of ahimsa one could, of course, become obsessive about the meaning of "to do no harm" and begin to equate washing microorganisms off one's hands, or eating a carrot, with killing. This kind of obsession, however, would probably distract one from the spirit of an ethic of nonviolence.

Experienced spiritual practitioners articulate two levels of exis-tence — one is absolute, or unconditional, in which no distinctions are made. All exist equally within the "One Mind," whether microor-ganism, carrot, or sentient being. We spend our days, however, living on the relative level, where we make distinctions within a hierarchy of events and values. We live on these two levels simultaneously, although we are much more aware of the relative level.

When operating on the relative level in our everyday life, we employ various standards to justify the discriminations and choices we must make. For most people, killing microorganisms, or a plant, is not the same as killing a sentient being. One is a creature with a ner-vous system, who enjoys a certain complexity and richness of life. The others are also life forms, and as such have their own vitality, but they reside at a lower level of existence. At the absolute level, of course, all differentiation disappears.

For most of us, then, the directive "do no harm" offers clear instructions about how to act, think, and feel. But ahimsa, elegant in its simplicity, exacts more from us than many are able to give. Speaking for myself, when I try to practice this dictate, my very human frailties invariably appear, diminishing my ability to respond as I had hoped. I regularly place barriers between my intent to honor the spirit of ahimsa and my fulfillment of that intent. This gap between intent and achievement reminds me that ahimsa is as much a process as a goal, and that by engaging in the process we point ourselves in the direction of greater awareness. Luckily, ahimsa becomes manifest in simple acts, not grand gestures. It does not require spiritual pyrotechnics or unusual powers. Whatever shortcomings we suffer from, we always can return to nonviolence — with each breath, thought, and expression.

Stephanie Kaza, who writes about Buddhism and ecology, describes an approach in which one may enjoy nondualistic, intimate contact with the natural world. In the precious moments when one catches a glimpse of the other — whether it is a parade of wild turkeys, a pair of black phoebes, or a baby great horned owl — one experiences two aspects of being: the ebb and flow of "twoness," as one communes with a specific and separate other, and that of "oneness" — "touching the unified field of energetic flux out of which all forms arise."[21] Through such intimate contact, after experiencing the "suchness," or the full exquisite beauty of another life, one can learn ahimsa. Through such encounters, one becomes less inclined to destroy fellow creatures in the web of life. As Kaza says, "It causes too much pain." Instead individuals become more compassionate, less aggressive, and better participants "in the 'big conversation.'"[22]

Animals can help us enter that "big conversation," but first we must notice them. Although we may not think of it this way, animals surround us at the supermarket, where they are made absent by language that renames their bodies as "food" and "cuisine." Through butchering, animals become what the feminist writer and activist Carol Adams calls "absent referents." She proposes, "The absent referent permits us to forget about the animal as an independent entity; it also enables us to resist efforts to make animals present."[23] The language of the absent referent directs us away from looking at a lamb chop and seeing a lamb, a creature who had a distinct personality, as every animal does. The lamb, when alive, had her own interests and attachments, and sought to avoid pain and suffering. All of these qualities are lost to us, however, by the time an animal has been "processed" into food, not just by the butcher's saw, but by language as well. Most of us simply see a lamb chop, or a chicken breast, or a pork loin — a piece of meat, without character or history.

Carol Adams's initial experience of seeing beyond meat to the individual personality of the animal occurred in college, although she developed her theory of the "absent referent" fifteen years later.

Carol grew up in a small, rural town in upstate New York, where she rode her beloved pony, Jimmy. She, her sisters, and a group of girl-friends would ride their ponies together, exploring the town and playing hide-and-seek. This was an enchanting time for Carol and her friends; they felt a close bond and a special relationship with their equine companions. After many years of enjoying these expeditions, Carol left for college while Jimmy remained boarded at her family's residence. In the summer of 1972, after her first year at Yale Divinity School, Carol returned home to visit before leaving for England, where she would work at Westminster Abbey. While upstairs, packing for her trip, Carol heard a frantic knocking at the house's side door. Opening the door, she found her neighbor coming to tell her that someone had just shot Jimmy. Carol raced out of the house barefoot and up the path to the pasture, where her pony lay dead. She knelt down beside him, holding him, and frantically wondering how this had happened. The village police officer, who had been called to the scene by her father, couldn't find an entry wound. Jimmy's death remained a mystery. He either died of a heart attack when he heard the shooting or, if he was shot, the entry wound had sealed over.

It didn't matter to Carol how he died, only that he had. Grief-stricken, she reluctantly left Jimmy's side to return to her house. In an attempt to soothe his daughter, Carol's father invited one of her girl-friends, Susie, who also had a horse, over for dinner that night. Susie's horse had just lost a foal, who had been born dead. The family cooked some hamburgers for dinner, typical fare for them at the time. As Carol recalled, she was about to take the third bite of her hamburger when the image of Jimmy's body lying in the pasture flashed in her mind. Suddenly she realized, "I am eating a dead cow. I would never eat Jimmy." She felt a total "aesthetic and moral revulsion." She continued to think about the connection she had just made. "Had I known this cow, I wouldn't eat the cow . . . this was death, too." As a result of this epiphany, Carol put the hamburger down, refused to eat any more of it, and eventually became a vegetarian. She didn't realize it at the time, but her life and spiritual direction had been irrevocably changed.[24]

Carol's empathic connection with Jimmy enabled her to restore the "absent referent." Instead of a hamburger, she now saw the individuality of a cow. In restoring the "absent referent," we become aware of an animal's life and in that awareness we have the opportunity to put ahimsa into practice.

Ahimsa can be practiced in a variety of ways and circumstances: in taking direct action to protect animals; in choosing the food we eat, the clothes we wear, or the household products we buy; in appreciating the nature of animals; and in our attitudes toward the animals with whom we have a relationship. The animals in our lives, and the many animals that surround our lives, offer us a "skillful means" to enact ahimsa and to make the fact of interbeing not just an ideal but a felt actuality in our lives.

Chapter Six

The Souls and Spiritual Lives
of Animals

Spirit Animals

Gary Kowalski has observed that as a clergyman he has license to consider such weighty issues as animals' souls and the sacredness of life — topics that many might view as too obscure, or elusive, even to contemplate. "The danger here is that we are often in over our heads," he wisely notes. "But at least we are swimming in deep water and out of the shallows."[1]

I am quite certain that Gary Kowalski wouldn't restrict consideration of such topics to the clergy, so following his lead, I would like to swim out into deep water and contemplate the souls and spiritual lives of animals. In order to enjoy a spiritual relationship with animals we must examine not only our own spiritual natures but theirs as well. Animals' spiritual lives, of course, are different from ours. They cannot create language, music, art, or religious traditions to express their spiritual feelings. They may not even be able to identify a particular experience as spiritual.

They may, however, possess certain spiritual advantages we do not.

Unable to employ symbolism and metaphor, they enjoy a more direct, unmediated experience with the divine. Lacking self-consciousness, they don't erect barriers, as we do, between themselves and the sacred. They live in the "isness of being" that many of us struggle to achieve, inhabiting sacred realms naturally and without effort. There are numerous accounts of an animal's participation in a spiritual process; let us turn to one now:

Two women, Sara and Lani, enjoyed the companionship of their beloved dog, Hattie, who easily fit the pattern of their lives. When Hattie was still quite young — about five years old — they discovered that she had an inoperable, and ultimately fatal, brain tumor. As Hattie's illness progressed, her functioning deteriorated. Once her back legs became paralyzed, Sara and Lani recognized that her time was limited, so they decided to take her on one last trip to all of the places she loved. As a golden retriever, Hattie especially cherished the ocean. Undeterred by the winter weather, the two women took Hattie to the sea, a few hours from their home. As they approached the coast, Hattie showed all her usual signs of excited interest: rapidly wagging tail, head up and sniffing, eyes gleaming, and what appeared to be a smiling face.

Once they found access to the ocean Sara and Lani parked the car and carried Hattie to the beach. They placed her gently on the sand; Hattie then dragged herself with her two front legs to the water's edge. She lay facing the sea, perhaps remembering all the pleasure she had experienced in water or contemplating unknown mysteries. As Sara and Lani watched her looking toward the horizon, they felt reassured by Hattie's calm.

Because it was winter, besides their three lone figures, the beach was empty. Then, in the distance, the two women noticed the first faint glimmer of something moving. As it approached, they saw it was a yellow lab, trotting up the beach with purpose. When he reached Hattie, he lay down beside her, and joined in her reverie. The two dogs lay side by side for quite a while, all the time gazing out at the ocean.

As the day came to a close, Sara and Lani retrieved Hattie from the water's edge. They carried her back to their van, with the yellow lab accompanying them the whole way. Once they reached the van, they offered the lab some food and water, which he refused. (Who has ever met a dog who refused a cookie?) He watched as they loaded up and prepared to leave. As they pulled out of their parking space, Sara and Lani turned to see what had happened to the yellow lab. He had disappeared as mysteriously as he had appeared. Driving away, Sara and Lani felt comforted by the yellow lab's visit, although at the time, they didn't know why.

Six days after the ocean trip, Hattie died. After her death, Sara and Lani learned that some people claim to have encountered "spirit dogs" who have come to accompany a dying animal. These "spirit dogs" do not eat or drink; their mission is to help a dying animal in the transition from life to death. Sara and Lani don't need to hear the many arguments for animal souls. They believe they participated in the direct experience of animal spirituality.

Most people today have never heard of spirit dogs, but this was not so for ancient people. In many cultures, dogs were closely associated with the spirit world. For example, the Ainu of Japan believed that dogs had the ability to detect ghosts, while the Inca of Peru believed that the howling of a dog predicted the death of a relative. The Parasee custom of bringing a dog to a dying person's side was based on the belief that the dog could help the dying person pass to the "other side." Many of these ancient stories explore the ways in which spirit dogs accompany human souls after death.[2] The story of Hattie, a rich addition to this mythology, shows us that spirit dogs serve their own kind as well as their human companions.

Dogs, of course, are not the only animals who have been associated with the spirit world. In our own country, we find extensive symbolic use of animals in Native American cultures. Each species of animal is characterized by their own meaningful spiritual attributes — rabbits by their quiet nonassertiveness, or eagles by their power to act as a conduit between humans and the supernatural. Perhaps the most significant symbol for the Plains Indians is the buffalo, whose spirit would lead those dancing the sun dance into supernatural visionary experiences.3

Throughout the history of art we also find animals as symbols of the divine and the sacred. From renderings of animals in cave art from 35,000 to 12,000 years ago in southwestern France and northern Spain to present-day modern art, artists have expressed their fascination with the spiritual nature of animals. Animals are frequently the subjects in the paintings of American artist Morris Graves. At an exhibition of his work a number of years ago, I ambled through the museum, enjoying the sense of mystery his art evokes. At one point I turned a corner and discovered a painting of a dove encircled in moonlight. Without deliberation, I uttered an involuntary gasp and thought, "There is God." My reaction surprised me, since I struggle constantly with the "if" and "what" of God. If persisting in the face of chronic doubt is a sign of faith, then I am indeed faithful. It's hard to describe what evoked my reaction, since I didn't arrive at this insight through any cognitive, rational process. Some quality of the dove literally "grabbed" me: her stillness; a transcendent, yet embodied, consciousness radiating from her; the ineffable sacred.

The "Cosmic Egg"

In Eastern religions, such as Hinduism and Buddhism, the doctrine of the interdependence of all life forms the basis for belief. This can be seen in the opening stanza of the Ishopanishad, a Hindu text: "The entire universe and everything in it, animate and inanimate, is His. Let us not covet anything. Let us treat everything around us reverently, as custodians. We have no charter for dominion. All wealth is commonwealth. Let us enjoy but neither hoard nor kill. The humble frog has as much right to live as we."4

The Sanskrit symbol of the "cosmic egg" captures the central unity of all life and the nondualistic nature of reality espoused by Eastern traditions. Eastern religions do not separate human and nonhuman animals the same way Judeo-Christian traditions do. In contrast, Eastern religions assign animals spiritual attributes, emphasize greater kinship between humans and nonhuman animals, and tend to give them greater moral consideration. Their emphasis on the nondualistic nature of reality tends to reorient humans, locating us not at the center or apex of existence, but rather within a larger context of interdependence — or interbeing as described by the Zen monk Thich Nhat Hanh.[5] We humans, according to Eastern traditions, are one group of beings among many others.

For example, *Devatas*, or deities, populate Hindu mythology. Every one of these, major or minor, presides over a specific function. The *vahana* or vehicle — the concrete visual representation of the deities — are usually derived from the world of animals. This resemblance between the deities and animals underscores their kinship, and exemplifies the integration of animal into the Eastern worldview.

The related Hindu concepts of *aham brahmasmi* — "I am not this body but, rather, I am spirit soul" — and reincarnation reinforce the view of animals as soulful creatures.[6] Although the bodies we "wear" come in many different forms — human, elephant, zebra, gorilla, dog, snake, bird — our essence is spirit. As spirit we are all one, all parts of God. Hindus neither identify themselves, or other living creatures, with the external body; instead, "they see the same eternal soul within each bodily shell, imbued with the same spiritual perfection."[7]

An example of this comes from a story about an interaction between "the Holy Mother," the wife of the noted Hindu holy man and avatar Ramakrishna, and her young niece. Revered in her own right, the Holy Mother was known for her boundless compassion and unlimited love. One day as she and her niece strolled down a path together, the young girl saw an ant traveling toward her. Thoughtlessly she reached over to squash the ant under her thumb.

The Holy Mother restrained her, saying, "Can you not see the divine in this creature? Let us revere it!"

Swami Vivekananda, the disciple of Ramakrishna responsible for bringing Vedanta to the United States, in speaking about animals' souls, wrote: "If we have a soul, so have they, and if they have none, neither have we. It is absurd to say that man alone has a soul, and the animals have none."[8] Whether we are ant or human, holy woman or sinner, Hindu or agnostic, the divine resides within each of us.

Transmigration, or reincarnation, which is central to Hindu and Buddhist thought, reinforces the concept of the "cosmic egg," that is, the unity of reality and the interdependence of existence. The Vedas, an ancient Hindu text, describes how each soul transmigrates through the bodies of different species. Usually a soul can only achieve liberation from repeated incarnations by assuming a human form, since these traditions believe that only humans have the necessary rational capacity to achieve illumination; in Buddhism such liberation from rebirth is enlightenment.

The interweaving of human and nonhuman existences, found in Hinduism and other Eastern traditions, extends to evolutionary theory as well as to the reincarnation of individual souls. According to Dr. Karan Singh, former Indian ambassador to the United States, the Vaishnava tradition of Hinduism symbolizes the evolution of life on this planet as represented by a series of divine incarnations that begin with fish, move to amphibians, then mammals, and finally to human incarnations. He states, "This view clearly holds that man...evolved out of these forms and is therefore integrally linked to the whole of creation."[9]

Although Buddhism does not espouse the presence of a soul as Hinduism does, reincarnation, or rebirth, is a central concept. The Jakata stories, parables about the Buddha's previous animal and human lives, illustrate the higher status assigned to animals in Buddhism. In these stories, all creatures have passed through many incarnations and inhabited many different forms — and all will pass through many more. All of us possess an animal nature since each of us has experienced countless rebirths, up and down the six realms articulated by Buddhism. (These six realms are, in ascending order: hell, hungry ghosts, animals, fighting demons, human beings, and heavenly beings.) To destroy an animal for food, for fur, or for any purpose whatsoever, is to destroy a part of ourselves. Buddhism holds, then, a deeply rooted belief that Buddhahood is latent in all creatures.

This belief, and the significance of reincarnation, are demonstrated in the practice of giving the precepts — a ceremony in which the recipient commits herself to a Buddhist code of ethical conduct — to an animal. Precepts are given to animals out of the desire to elevate their consciousness so that they may achieve a more favorable rebirth and in time achieve full liberation. According to Zen Master Dogen, founder of the Soto School of Zen, "Those who experience this communion [with Buddha] inevitably take this refuge [in the Three Treasures of Buddha, Dharma, and Sangha] whether they find themselves as celestial or human beings, dwellers in hell, hungry ghosts, or animals."[10]

The Eastern religious concept that one may have assumed various nonhuman animal forms in previous lifetimes — and might well inhabit animal form in the future — is a radical belief we should not overlook. Certainly we would alter our treatment of animals if we truly believed that we or someone we love had taken, or might one day take, animal form. And, if we believe in reincarnation across species, we no longer can view animals as "other." The radical disconnection long maintained by most of Western thought dissolves. We would no longer think in terms of gross dichotomies but rather in a flowing, dynamic continuum. They would be us and we would be them.

Buddhist and Hindu perspectives do not deny the differences between human and nonhuman animals. Both traditions propose that the human realm offers the greatest opportunity for spiritual evolution. (Buddhism and Hinduism agree that the ultimate spiritual attainment is escaping rebirth. For the Hindu, this achievement leads to a state of seamless unity with the divine; for Buddhists, on the other hand, it is the realization of emptiness.) The nondualistic approaches of both traditions emphasize the continuity of being.

Doctrines such as reincarnation encourage us to focus on the unity and continuity of creation, which in turn allow us to heighten our awareness and develop our compassion. By avoiding artificial divisions between ourselves and other living creatures, we can transcend the limits of our individual experiences. Then we are open to a central reality in which we may know the absolute, or the "One Mind without distinctions of any kind."[11] Developing awareness of our kinship with animals can open the door to this other world of possibility, in which one unites, at the deepest level, with the sacred.

The enlightened have no trouble recognizing the divinity in all creatures, as illustrated by a story about Ramakrishna. As Ramakrishna was performing a worship service in a temple, a cat wandered in just when he was about to offer food to the deity. Upon seeing the cat, Ramakrishna bowed down and gave the cat the food. Many people gasped in horror. As the writer Isherwood notes, however, Ramakrishna had perfectly illustrated what Vedanta is all about.

Nephesh, or Animal Souls, in the Judeo-Christian Tradition

Many authors have demonstrated ample biblical support for the position that animals have souls. The Hebrew word *nephesh* — that which animates living beings with personality, desire, feelings, and volition, what we know as soul — refers to both animals and humans throughout the Hebrew Bible. The New Testament uses *psuche*, the Greek counterpart to nephesh, to refer to animals' souls. (Rev. 8:9, 16:3).

The ancient Israelites based their conclusions about animal souls on their observations of, and interactions with, the animals with whom they lived in close proximity. We can infer from the use of nephesh to refer to both human and animal souls that they recognized the similarity between the two. On the basis of their intimate knowledge of animals, they understood thousands of years ago what the disciplines of cognitive ethology, animal behaviorism, and anthropology have only documented in the last twenty years: Animals think, feel, desire, pursue interests, express preference, plan, and calculate — and some even show self-awareness. In other words, animals enjoy all of the attributes that comprise soul.

Numerous other passages in the Bible suggest God's concern for animals. The Hebrew Bible speaks about animals' affinity to God (Ps. 148:7–10, 150:6), declares that animals will be present in eternity (Isa. 65:25, Rev. 5:13–14), and confirms that they can be redeemed by God (Eph. 1:10; Col. 1:20). Both animals and humans mourn before God (Jonah 3:6–9) and look toward God for sustenance (Ps. 104:27–31) and deliverance (Rom. 8:18–23).[12]

J. R. Hyland, another theologian who writes about religion and animals, observes that the biblical passage describing the flood is unique in its use of repetition. Five different scripture passages refer to a covenant relationship that God enters not just with humans but also with nonhuman animals. This repetition signals the importance of establishing a special and sacred connection between God and animals.[13]

Despite the fact that nephesh refers to both human and nonhuman animal souls, and other references in the Bible address animals' spiritual status, for the most part, mainstream Judeo-Christian thought ignores or rejects the spiritual significance of animals.

Very few Western theologians have seriously addressed the question of animal afterlife. Some, such as C. S. Lewis, hesitated because they feared their colleagues' censure. Lewis admitted to being leery of approaching the topic, lest he find himself "in the company of the old maids."[14] He feared appearing sentimental, that his interest in animals would open him to mockery. Of course this traditional association of women with emotionality and animals has served to demean both parties and to dismiss the importance of deep feelings in making spiritual and moral judgments.

C. S. Lewis's imagined critics might have cited a number of complex reasons for their dismissal of animals as spiritual beings. Some writers propose that the monotheistic emphasis on a transcendent God distances the divine from earthly existence. And the influence of Aristotle, who promulgated a hierarchy in which humans possessed the right to "use" animals because of their position at the top of the hierarchy, permeates Western thought.

In Christianity, the subject of animal souls is interwoven with the religious concept of redemption and the philosophical concept of self-awareness. Much of Christian thought has argued that animals cannot reason, and if they cannot reason, they cannot be self-aware. Without self-awareness, the thinking goes, they cannot possess souls and enjoy an afterlife. If animals merely experience a succession of sensations, with no sense of "I," how could they even recognize themselves in an afterlife?

Other theologians have contended that because animals are not moral agents they cannot enjoy an afterlife. If one accepts the proposition that animals are not capable of morality, one also must conclude that they cannot "sin." Unlike us, this argument goes, animals are truly innocent. Why, then, wouldn't this innocence make them more likely to experience God's grace, rather than exclude them from it?

The theologian Stephen Webb wisely notes that the kind of reasoning that prevents animals from enjoying an afterlife only holds up if one imagines heaven as a place of reward and punishment. What if heaven is about redemption and consolation? Webb points to a passage in Revelations stating that heaven is a place where "God shall wipe away all their tears." Clearly animals share in the suffering of the world. "What if heaven allows for the completion of what is left incomplete in this life?" Webb writes. "This would connect the afterlife to the notion of justice, not the psychology of the fear of death and the desire for more living and infinite pleasure."[15] Theologian Jay

McDaniel picks up on this notion that redemption is not about eternal life but rather about those creatures who died in an incomplete state being made whole.[16]

The argument offered by theologians and philosophers that animals cannot reason, and that morality requires the ability to reason, has clearly divided humans from other species. The argument also fails on many accounts. First, animals do employ a kind of reasoning, although not exactly like human reasoning. Scientists such as Donald Griffin, Jane Goodall, Roger Fouts, Diane Savage-Rumbaugh, and others, have carefully documented examples of animal reasoning. Most recently, neuroscientists at the University of California at Los Angeles have discovered that monkeys possess an innate ability to conceptualize numbers and can be taught to count at least to the number nine. While earlier research had been criticized for not clearly determining whether the animals had actually learned to count, or had merely learned by rote or simply recognized certain visual patterns, reviewers expressed confidence that this research design overcame the weaknesses of previous experiments. The University of California researchers remain uncertain whether or not the two monkeys in the experiment could add or subtract, but they are certain that the monkeys understood the sophisticated concepts of "twoness" and "threeness."[17]

By now it should be clear that the ability to reason is not a discrete trait that one has or doesn't have. Reasoning is rather a continuum with a myriad of different qualities. Dogs do not reason like elephants, and tigers do not reason like humans. But all exercise some degree, and type, of reasoning. This scientific evidence of animal intelligence knocks away the foundation of the Western rejection of animal souls. Animals do reason, enjoy consciousness, and therefore meet the standards presented by Western religious thought for having souls and being eligible for redemption.

Luckily, even before modern science, free thinkers relied on their own experiences and logic rather than the sometimes tortured theological reasoning of their faiths. St. Francis of Assisi, probably the best-known Christian figure associated with animals, demonstrated an attunement to animals and nature that caught the attention of the people around him. He was said to possess uncanny powers that tamed people-eating wolves and drew birds to listen to his preaching. Whether he actually exercised magical capacities is not important. What is important is that St. Francis exhibited a sensitivity that animals immediately recognized. He was a man animals could trust, whom they didn't have to fear. St. Francis provides a welcome antidote, as Michael Fox writes, to the "profane and dualistic beliefs of human superiority and separateness from the rest of Nature...."[18]

St. Francis rescued bleating lambs on their way to slaughter, removed worms from danger on a busy road, and preached to the birds. Like a good Buddhist or Hindu, he recognized that every living creature shares consciousness. St Francis's habit of speaking to animals as though they could understand, of course, is not that unusual. What human caretaker of an animal does not talk to her or his companion? I enjoy daily conversations with my two dogs. I also find myself talking to birds. As I walked to my car recently, I stopped to listen to some lively "caws" coming from some large, black crows perched high in a tree above me. It grew out of a lone patch of green dotting the large parking lot I was crossing. "Hello there!" I called to the crow. "And how are you today?" The birds paused; I like to think they were listening to me. Whether they were or not, their cawing and my appreciation were a welcome reminder that we are part of nature. Sometimes it's hard to remember amidst our urban life, but they cawed me back to this comforting reality.

John Wesley, the founder of Methodism and Bishop of London in 1747, was inspired by the idea of the peaceable kindom to become a vegetarian. In addition to becoming a vegetarian for health and spiritual reasons, he also advocated the existence of animal souls. In his sermon "The General Deliverance," Wesley argued that all of creation, including animals, will be restored — not only to their previous states but "to a far higher degree than they ever enjoyed." Although Wesley did not believe that God held animals in the same regard as humans, he contended that God's redemption of animals was a way to make "amends for all they suffer while under their present bondage."[19] We can only hope he was right.

Letting Animals Speak for Themselves

Perhaps the simplest, most fruitful way to appreciate the spiritual lives of animals is to let them speak for themselves. As many authors before me have noted, animals communicate with us, if we only stop to listen.

Sometimes it is not until a pet dies that we become open to an experience we might otherwise disregard. Jan, a friend of mine, had an aged but beloved dog, Beau, who suffered from crippling arthritis. As she observed Beau's increasing difficulty moving, she asked her vet how she would know when it was time to relieve Beau of his distress. The vet, trusting the depth of Jan's relationship with Beau, said, "You'll know." And he was right; Jan did. When that time came, she carried Beau in her arms to the veterinarian's office. After she gently placed Beau on the table, the vet, whom Beau knew quite well by now, administered the drug that would end his life. Jan was right next to Beau, holding him, talking to him, and stroking him.

As his life left him, Jan said she saw a rush of energy leave Beau's body, exiting through his mouth. In trying to describe this profound yet indescribable experience, she said she didn't exactly "see" as much as experience the energy. All the same, she knew with certainty what had happened.

Was this Beau's soul taking flight? Was his consciousness now transforming into the next phase of its existence? We don't know, of course. I have been well schooled to be skeptical of such speculations. Recently, however, I have been influenced by the Eastern religions that one's consciousness transforms itself after death — either into another life form, or into a land "beyond the samsaric suffering world," where one will find a final peace.

A writer in the yoga tradition notes that no one doubts that they were born, although they do not remember their birth. Yet many Westerners scoff at the idea of reincarnation. We know from modern physics that energy does not "disappear," but becomes transformed. So why not the energy of our consciousness? Ayang Rinpoche, from the Tibetan Buddhist tradition, explains, "At the time of death, our consciousness ordinarily leaves our body through one of the nine doors; the two eyes, two nostrils, mouth, two ears, and two lower openings."[20] It appears that Beau's consciousness exited through his mouth.

Some doubters might say that Jan saw what she wanted to see and dismiss her experience as wishful thinking. It is harder to discredit evidence of an animal's consciousness when someone who has had no relationship with the companion animal, or more than one person, perceives it. Scott Smith, author of *Pet Souls: Evidence that Animals Survive Death*, has collected such stories from hundreds of people. One witness of an animal "soul" was a veterinarian who had come to treat a white horse sick with colic. As she tended to the ailing creature, she noticed another white horse in the same large corral. After examining the horse, she met with the human caretakers to give them instructions for his treatment. She cautioned them to separate the two white horses so that the ill horse's fecal matter could be identified and analyzed. They look puzzled as she said this, since they only had one horse. As the vet described the second horse, the caretakers said that it fit the description of an older horse of theirs who had recently died. They wondered if the deceased horse had returned to watch over his sick companion.

Another way to discount such experiences is to call them hallucinations. Of course, they could be just that. But they could also be something else. It is harder to explain it away when more than one person witnesses an animal "ghost," as shown in the following story:

In a town near the Austrian border, twin ten-year-old boys were swimming in the frigid water of Lake Constance. When they both began to flounder, their father swam out to rescue them. Before he could reach them he witnessed the family's collie, Fritz, who had been dead for a year, by their side. Fritz guided them safely to the beach. But as the onlookers rushed to their side, Fritz disappeared. It wasn't just the father who had seen Fritz, but about a dozen eyewitnesses. The police report of this incident confirmed the account.[21]

Some stories concern dogs who come back as "ghosts"; other times it is the dog who perceives the ghost. Gary Kowalski observes that at unexpected times, the fur on an animal's back may bristle, or they peer off into space intently or utter a gutteral moan for no apparent reason. He supposes that they, like us, have a sense of the mysterious and that one aspect of this mysterious is, as the philosopher Rudolf Otto suggests, "...[a] sense of the uncanny, the eerie...the overwhelming mystery of existence."[22]

If one has a creation-centered spirituality, as opposed to a human-centered one, then the idea of animals' souls and spiritual lives seems quite reasonable. In a creation-centered spirituality — or to use McDaniel's phrase, ecological spirituality — nonhuman animals are not spiritually distinct from human animals. The mystical traditions understand this; their stories often describe a kinship with all creatures and a oneness with creation. The holy person often enjoys the ability to acutely share the experiences of another creature — to live in their skin, so to speak. One story from the *Legend of the Baal-Shem* describes it this way: "He who thus serves in perfection has conquered the primeval duality.... He dwells in the kingdom of life, and yet all walls have fallen, all boundary-stones are uprooted, all separation is destroyed. *He is the brother of the creatures and feels their glance as if it were his own, their step as if his own feet walked, their blood as if it flowed through his own body.*" (italics added)[23]

Fundamentally, it really makes little difference if animals possess the ability to "return" after their deaths, or to see things we cannot perceive, or to commune with the spirit world. What is really important is that animals are who they are — beings who enjoy life, grieve at loss, enjoy beauty, participate in social networks, and love. As we engage in a relationship with animals, and learn to appreciate their unique qualities, we experience awe for the wonders, and interdependence, of existence. We learn to love not only them but all of creation.

Animals only have to be themselves, and we have to be smart enough to pause and appreciate them for who they are. Cleveland Amory, the acclaimed writer who started The Fund for Animals in 1967, championed the protection of animals throughout his life. Of all his achievements, perhaps the one closest to his heart was the Black Beauty Ranch, which he founded in the vast, sprawling plains of Texas. Black Beauty provides a place where animals who have been rescued from abuse and slaughter can safely spend the rest of their lives in an environment designed to allow them to live as naturally as possible.

Cleveland died recently at age eighty-one. After his funeral and cremation, his friends debated the most appropriate place to spread his ashes. After some lively discussion, they arrived at what each of them immediately recognized as the right thing to do.

One of Black Beauty's inhabitants was Friendly, one of the many burros the fund has rescued from slaughter. Cleveland and Friendly were particularly good friends, and whenever Cleveland visited the ranch, Friendly would spend time with him. Both enjoyed each other, as can readily be seen in one photograph of them, which shows Friendly nuzzling up to Cleveland and Cleveland leaning into him with a warm smile. Cleveland's friends decided to put his ashes in a bag, which they tied around Friendly's neck. They poked holes in the bag so that as the burro walked Cleveland's ashes would be distributed around the ranch he loved. As this loving story illustrates, to the end of our individual existences and beyond, animals can participate in the meaningful moments of our lives.

Chapter Seven

The Parallel Worlds of Human and Nonhuman Animals

In this chapter, you will meet Eve, who like many of us strives to be good and spiritually responsible, and to instill meaning in her life. Eve happens to be a woman, but she could be either gender, any race, nationality, religion, or social class. What is important is that she is a seeker. For one short day we will observe Eve through the perspective of two parallel worlds: the one she occupies as she goes about her daily life, making many of the ordinary decisions all of us make; and the lesser-known world of the animals whose lives are affected by her decisions. When we meet her, Eve is not aware of the animal world. Like Eve, I spent most of my life unaware of this other world, in which millions of animals live and too often suffer needlessly. By observing Eve, I hope to open our awareness to this other world, which has been kept out of sight, although it is always present, right beside the one we know. By making the world of the animals visible, we gain insight — the first step on any spiritual journey.

Eve's Day

It was a day much like any other. Eve awoke happy enough, as was her habit. At fifty-five she had successfully navigated most of life's potential pitfalls, and she considered herself lucky. She was. Eve was content in her thirty-year marriage to Rob. Their two children, Ellen and David, were both married with families and well-established careers, and seemed secure. Every family, of course, has its difficulties, and Eve's family had not escaped the complications that humans seem to be so good at devising. Eventually her family managed to come through these difficulties with everybody intact and often more deeply connected to one another. Eve thought it was their positive outlook and expectation of successful resolutions that often saved them. During those troubled times, the characteristic optimism of Eve's family served as a beacon, lighting their path, so that they avoided the turbulent vortexes of emotion that destroy some families.

By the time Eve arose, Rob had been up for a good two hours. Always an early riser, he claimed that this habit came from growing up in a farm family, even though he had been a suburbanite for almost forty years now. He always raised this claim when gently teased by his family about his early morning habits. By now it was one of those jokes that can maintain, and sometimes restore, the affectionate ties between family members. They all realized, Rob included, that his early morning habits provided a tie to his past and gave him a comforting sense of solidity.

Eve stretched luxuriously before she pulled the covers aside, readying herself to enter the world. Enjoying the pleasant feeling in her body as it lengthened, she laughed out loud, thinking of her grandson, Josh. The other day when he was visiting with his mother, Ellen, they had found him intently talking to Pepper, the family dog. At twenty months, Josh had not yet realized that try as he might, Pepper would never be able to converse with him in the same language. But there he was, brow knit earnestly, fingers wiggling with expression, pouring his heart out to Pepper, who sat "listening" politely. Pepper, a dalmatian by birth and a diplomat by nature, had a remarkable capacity for calm and sincere responses to the most unexpected activities of her human family. Despite her tendency to shed profusely with the changes of season, Pepper's family loved her and she returned their love with her unconditional love and devotion.

When they noticed this one-sided conversation between Josh and Pepper, both Ellen and Eve were delighted. Eve could feel that same delight as she remembered the scene this morning. Putting on her slippers, ready to make her way to the bathroom, she wondered why Josh's efforts at cross-species communication were so heartwarming. Was it because of Josh's ignorance of limits? Or was it that all of us long to overcome communication barriers, and Josh was still innocent enough to think he could?

Eve continued to muse as she began what she called her "morning ablutions." Ever since her children were old enough to go to school and she had more of the morning to herself, Eve took time to enjoy the ritual of cleansing her body and preparing it for the day. Like Rob's early morning habits, Eve's linked her to something familiar and reassuring.

She squinted in the mirror, noticing the growing number of gray hairs, which seemed to increase at the same rate as her difficulty in seeing them without her contacts. "Ah, well," Eve thought, "the alternative to growing old isn't very appealing." She didn't need her contacts to locate the hormones she had begun taking four years ago to replace those her body no longer produced on its own. Organized in daily increments in a pill separator that Eve kept by the side of the sink, Eve's eyes were still good enough to see the "S" marking the last place on the container, indicating it was Saturday, and the end of the week. Eve couldn't decide if her methodical approach to life was the reason she became a librarian, or the result of thirty years of systematizing, organizing, and cataloging. Whatever their origin, she and her family enjoyed the benefits of her organizational skills. Every morning, as soon as she washed her hands, Eve took her Premarin. Swallowing this tiny bit of estrogen that she hoped would help her avoid the cardiovascular diseases that ran in her family was by now so automatic that Eve did it without a conscious thought. This morning was no different.

The pregnant mare that produced Eve's estrogen was one of 80,000 horses who are tethered in stalls every year throughout North Dakota and Canada. When October arrives, a mare is impregnated, which produces high concentrations of estrogen in her urine. Then she is placed "on line." The mare's life "on line" lasts about six months and will end, temporarily, when the estrogen in her urine decreases and she is ready to give birth.

During this time, she will spend most of her days standing on a cement floor, with no bedding, in a stall four feet wide and five feet long. She will have little opportunity to lie down. She will be attached to a contraption that catches her urine, which is then processed to become Premarin, Eve's morning pill. Her legs will swell from the edema that results from constantly standing on the hard floor; she will also probably develop thrush, a painful foot infection. She will be given water from a timed water machine, but she will probably not get as much as she needs, because a lack of water raises the estrogen levels in her urine.

After she gives birth, the mare and her foal will be allowed to pasture together for six months. When October first approaches again the mare and foal will be separated, and the mare impregnated again and put back "on line." After the foals are separated from their mothers, they will be shipped to the slaughterhouse in a cramped double-decker truck with metal flooring. At the end of this trip they will be killed and their flesh sold to Europe and Japan for human consumption. In Canada alone, about 400,000 horses are killed every year for this purpose.

This cycle will continue every year for twelve or fourteen years, the average life expectancy of a Premarin mare. Well-tended domesticated horses live for twenty to thirty years. Horses are strong, agile, and athletic animals. They need to move. In natural settings, horses wander and forage for up to twenty hours a day, munching fresh grass, running, and interacting with other horses.[1]

Eve flicked on the radio as she put in her contacts and prepared to brush her teeth. She often listened to her local National Public Radio station. Listening intently to a conversation between an NPR commentator and the author of a book on children and poverty, Eve heard the author describe the appalling conditions in which so many children live, and his view that society and government have turned their back on these children. Eve felt a tug at her heart. Whenever she heard about suffering, especially the suffering of innocents, she cringed. Eve made a mental note to raise this issue of children and poverty with the town council to see if it could be addressed. She did not expect miracles, but she did want to know what programs were available to poor children in her area. The conversation on the radio, and the one that Eve was having inside her head, ended just as she finished the cleansing part of her ritual. Now for the artistic process of applying her makeup. Although it was Saturday, she put on a little makeup because she had errands to run. Eve saw applying makeup as a small way to express her creativity. As she finished, she could hear Pepper barking a greeting from her favorite spot in the backyard to some of the neighborhood children. Eve walked down the stairs wondering what kind of tea she would drink before taking Pepper out for a walk and running her errands. It was a sunny autumn morning and she looked forward to the day that awaited her.

Every item Eve used that morning had been tested on animals — the soap she used to wash her hands and face, her toothpaste, and her makeup, which consisted of moisturizer, foundation, rouge, and a touch of mascara. Eve's hand lotion, hair gel, and perfume were also tested. The animals used for this part of Eve's morning ritual included four rabbits, three rats, and two guinea pigs.

A lab worker placed a rabbit, chosen to test some of the ingredients in Eve's mascara, in a restraining device. Even though the product was a known irritant, with an alcohol content of 82 percent, it was dripped in the rabbit's eyes. (Some rabbits have the tested substances injected into their vaginas.) The rabbit was given repeated applications for the next three days producing ulceration, pockets of pus, and swelling. The lab technician would record the injury incurred, what dosages had produced what kinds of damage and over what period of time. Often the testing companies don't give local anesthetics to the animals; they fear pain relievers might obscure their results, although it is not clear that this is the case. After completing the experiment, the lab worker killed the rabbit. Sometimes those who kill the rabbits do so expertly and quickly; but when the lab workers are unskilled, or rushed, the animals sometimes experience a painful and prolonged death — or autopsies are performed on them while still living. The rest of the animals used to test Eve's cosmetics — the other rabbit, three rats, and a guinea pig — went through similar procedures and painful experiences. If Eve had shampooed her hair that morning, another animal would have been added to her list.[2]

As Eve put on the kettle for tea, Pepper scampered in to greet her. The family had observed that Pepper never just walked — she scampered, loped, galloped, or pranced. Pepper was born with an innate enthusiasm that could be infectious if one were in the right mood. However, if it was one of those days when the world seemed off-center, Pepper's ebullience — a too-real reminder of one's inferior state — could be quite annoying. Today it was definitely a pleasure to see her unbounded love for life. Eve looked down at Pepper, patted her on the head, and pointed to the dog bed that lay in a corner of the room. "Cool your jets, young lady," Eve told Pepper. "We'll go for our walk in a few minutes. First I need my tea."

Eve made her tea, half-read the newspaper, and half-planned the evening's meal. Her son, David, and his family were coming over for dinner. She made a mental checklist of what food she had in the house and what she would need to pick up. Sipping her last bit of tea, Eve went to the closet. Since it was a cool autumn day, she pulled out a coat she hadn't worn since last winter, her cool-weather, dog-walking parka. Mud-colored, it was perfect for being around dogs, who at any moment may imprint you with their canine footprints. Eve's parka had some kind of fur around the collar — at least she thought it was fur, although she couldn't really identify it. Being of a practical bent, Eve wasn't much of a fur fancier, but she remembered how it had been hard to find a parka like this one without some kind of trim. As she put on her coat — the signal — Pepper came to her with her leash in mouth.

The fur that trimmed the hood of Eve's parka came from a coyote that grew up in the American Southwest. Until his capture and death, when he was two years old, he had lived with his pack. They roamed about, doing what coyotes do: killing enough to feed themselves, relaxing in the sun, sleeping, grooming themselves, and — especially the pups — exploring and playing together. When the coyote was too young to hunt, and his parents were away finding food, one of his "uncles," an older male relative, watched him.

The coyote who was skinned for Eve's parka led a satisfying but uneventful life until the day he took a wrong turn and got caught in the steel jaws of a leg-hold trap. Animals often are trapped for days before death relieves their suffering. During the time they are ensnared they suffer from the pain of festering wounds, dehydration, hunger, and, of course, intense anxiety. Animals caught in traps desperately try to free themselves. Some resort to chewing off the trapped body part in order to break free — what trappers call a "wring off." For most, their only escape from the trap will be death, and the manner of death is typically brutal. In order to protect the integrity of the fur, animals in traps are not shot but clubbed or stomped to death.[3]

What Eve didn't realize is that wildlife in this country are subjected to greater cruelty than animals in other nations, such as those in Western Europe. The trapper who bludgeoned and stomped the coyote to death was not doing anything illegal. Few state laws restrict methods of killing. And while trapping and killing animals always involves pain and terror, the steel jaw leg-hold trap inflicts extreme cruelty. Although it is banned in Europe, the United States and Canada still allow it. This method of trapping claims not only the lives and limbs of its intended victims but also pet dogs and cats, golden eagles, swans, and human children — all seized by their steel jaws.[4]

After Eve slipped on her coat, she headed with Pepper in tow out the front door into the autumn sunshine. It felt good to walk. Their destination was the neighborhood dog park, a large patch of green that attracted dogs and their owners from miles around. Here they congregated every morning, especially on weekends. It took years before Eve learned the names of the dogs' human companions; for a long time she referred to this or that person as "Muggy's Mom" or "Brady's Dad."

This morning, as she did every Saturday, Eve focused on her

breath as she walked the mile to the dog park. It was her opportunity to focus her awareness, which she did by repeating a favorite prayer or hymn. By concentrating on something meaningful to her, she began to collect herself so that the zillions of thoughts that flew through her mind on any given day began to fade. She noticed an internal calmness; paradoxically she felt both more solid and more fluid. For Eve this was a spiritual exercise. It enabled her to get down to something very basic about her existence and about existence in general. Eve seemed better able to receive the energy she encountered on her walk with Pepper — the mothers and fathers with their children in strollers, homeowners raking leaves, the feel of the sun on her face, the glory of the fall colors on each passing tree.

Once at the park, Eve and Pepper knew what to do. Pepper played with her dog friends, and Eve chatted with their human escorts. Over the years Eve had developed a friendship with many of the "dog people," as they called one another. After Pepper had ample time to enjoy herself with her playmates, and Eve had chatted with her park friends, they happily headed back for the second stage of their Saturday outing. When they arrived home, Pepper hopped in the backseat of the car as Eve prepared to run her endless Saturday errands. Pepper's company kept Eve in better spirits, her constantly wagging tail helping Eve to keep a more positive perspective. With her trademark efficiency, Eve made her way to the grocery store, cleaners, office supply store, and then home.

After Eve had unloaded the groceries and Pepper, she decided to prepare as much of her dinner as she could before, so that she could feel relaxed and ready to enjoy David and his family when they arrived. Because they were celebrating David's recent promotion, she had planned a menu around his preferences. Then she and Rob had decided it would be fun to watch a video as a way for adults and children to share an activity together. Rob's job was to find a suitable video as part of his Saturday errands.

Eve thumbed through some of the latest issues of a gourmet

cooking magazine, looking for a new way to prepare the pork loin she had bought for dinner. She was familiar enough with the perfectly posed food in these pages to know that these photographs represented an ideal, rather than the reality she would achieve. But they usually tasted good, and that's what counted. Eve settled on a recipe that looked appealing and not too complicated. Getting down to work, Eve began rubbing the various spices into the pork loin, as directed by the recipe. She was careful to wash her hands as she moved from handling the pork to some other part of the kitchen. Eve was increasingly mindful of the microorganisms that lurked in some meat these days. She wanted to nourish her family, not kill them!

The pig butchered for Eve's pork loin was born and lived twenty weeks on a factory farm. That's the average lifespan of a male pig bred for slaughter. The average life span of a pig who escapes slaughter and lives in a sanctuary is ten to fifteen years. In factory farms pigs are taken away from their mothers at three weeks — ten to fourteen weeks short of a natural weaning cycle — then castrated without anesthetic. Next they are placed in a pen with a mesh-wire floor, crowded with other piglets, forced to live in a cramped, sterile environment. The only time they will be outdoors in when they are transferred from the factory farm to the truck bound for the slaughterhouse. As a result of this forced confinement, pigs may resort to cannibalism, tail-biting, or repetitively biting the large-gauge wire on the gate of the nursery pens. This behavior, which has been termed "porcine stress syndrome" by the factory farm industry, indicates extreme emotional distress. The lives of sows are even more tortured than those of the other pigs. They live in a state of constant confinement until repeated breeding exhausts them; then they are slaughtered.

On a typical trip to the slaughterhouse, pigs are steered onto overloaded trucks to make journeys of many hours. If it is a hot day, the pigs' body temperatures will soar since they are unable to sweat; many will die of heart attacks or suffocation. These corpses are then tossed into the pet food bins. Once they arrive at the slaughterhouse they are herded into a large area divided by gates into pens. They immediately hear the clanging of machinery, the hissing of power hoses, and the shrieks of doomed animals. The men who do the stunning are pressured to hurry, so they often cut corners and don't leave the electrical stunning device on long enough. It takes a minimum of seven seconds to effectively render a pig unconscious, but when rushed they only give it about one to two seconds. Some animals are alive when the men slit their throats, and they bleed to death.

In their natural environment, where they have freedom of movement, pigs spend about one-third of their day grazing, about one-fifth rooting, and another one-fifth interacting with the environment in other ways. A well-defined social order and close mother-piglet ties characterize pig society. Friendly creatures, they also develop bonds with human companions. Pigs can be very active, sometimes traveling up to thirty miles a day. They are highly intelligent animals, ranked just behind humans, other primates, and dolphins. If given a name, they will come when called; they'll often greet human strangers with curious friendliness.[5]

With her pork loin ready for the oven, Eve thumbed through her magazines for a dessert. One photo of a creamy custard with shades of glossy nut-brown looked spectacular. She felt her taste buds tingle with anticipation. "That's it," she thought. "I can put that together, too." A custard requires a lot of eggs, milk, and cream. Eve hesitated briefly at the custard's fat content but then defended her choice by reasoning that this was a celebratory dinner. With perfect timing, Rob appeared in the kitchen, his errands complete, just as Eve was putting the custard in the oven. Now they could pause over cups of hot tea, an interlude they both welcomed.

Laying chickens, like all factory farm animals, are subjected to miserable conditions while alive and a difficult death. Factory farms house up to half a million chickens, with four confined to a cage the size of an album cover, cages stacked on top of one another, row after tow. The male chicks, who are of no use, are thrown into a plastic bag when born, where they suffocate. A few days after birth the female chicks are debeaked without anesthetic, using a guillotine-like device; their toes are cut off to avoid becoming embedded in the wire mesh of the cages. Because of severe overcrowding, chickens develop bald patches and sores, as well as lung infections from the toxic fumes emitted from their waste, for which they are fed antibiotics. By the time they arrive at the slaughterhouse, 80 percent of their bones will be broken due to the calcium depletion caused by the strain of egg overproduction.[6]

Most dairy cows also live in conditions of intense confinement. They are placed either in "free-stall" holding barns, which allow them to move a few feet in either direction on concrete or slotted floors, or in "tie-stall" barns where they are kept stationary by chains around their necks. Lack of sunlight and overproduction often cause the cows to go lame. Dairy cows grazing in green pastures live productively for twelve to fifteen years; those confined to factory farms live two or three years and are slaughtered for hamburger meat.

Cows only produce milk for ten months after their calves' birth, so whether in a factory farm or not, they will be reimpregnated forty to sixty days after each birth. Calves are taken away at birth, with the females raised to produce milk and males for beef or veal. Newborn males who are placed in veal crates live in the harshest confinement. Chained at the neck, in a stall with no bedding or straw (they might eat it), they can barely move. They spend their entire fourteen- to sixteen-week lives in total darkness, except when lights are turned on at feeding time. When they are eventually taken to slaughter, they are often too weak to walk and have to be dragged to their destination.

Cattle who live freely have defined personalities, and are not the bored, passive, and hopeless creatures one might encounter on a factory farm. Some have been known to get down on their knees to inspect holes being dug for fence posts. Others chase dogs, or anything interesting that blows into their field — pieces of newspaper or stray balloons. One free cow spent her time looking for ways to escape her fencing; another would cuddle up with a human visitor, laying down next to anyone interested, and putting her large head in the visitor's lap. Throughout the day, free cows will "...dance around, playing with each other, circling and butting heads....They'll look for any excuse to run and kick their heels up."[7]

Eve and Rob lingered over their warm tea on this sunny, crisp autumn Saturday. After thirty years of marriage, they still enjoyed talking to one another. Pushing back their chairs, now ready to do more work after their brief respite together, Eve asked, "By the way, what video did you get for tonight?" Rob laughed, knowing the dinner menu: "Can you believe it? *Babe*, the movie about that pig!" Eve joined in his laughter. "Oh, well," she responded. "I know the kids will enjoy it." Rob left to keep his appointment with the town's planning committee, which was meeting to make a budget for a new environmental program for kids. "Before I do anything else, " Eve thought, looking around at the kitchen, "I'd better clean up this disaster area." With brisk efficiency, Eve rinsed dishes and placed them in the dishwasher, then wiped the countertops with a sponge soaked in a solution of bleach and water. Eve periodically cleaned her countertops this way; it made them sparkle, and also sanitized them since the bleach killed harmful bacteria.

One method for testing products on animals is the LD-50 test, also known as lethal dose-50. In this test a substance is injected down the throat of an animal, often with a stomach tube, to determine what dosage will kill 50 percent of the tested population within fourteen days. Often these substances are highly caustic, causing some animals to die immediately; others suffer from convulsions, labored breathing, diarrhea, and vomiting. Those alive after fourteen days are killed. As far back as 1978, an official study of the Royal Society of London condemned the LD-50 as having limited value; current research has found that the LD-50 test has a predictive value of 59 percent — low by any standard.[8] Scientific habit dies hard, however. Many of these tests are still used today, even though they are "less reliable and more costly than existing nonanimal tests."[9] When a combination of human cell tests are used rather than live animals, for example, the predictive value jumps to a respectable 80 percent. Human cell tests use cells from the particular organ(s) in question, providing more reliable results.[10]

Rats are commonly used for laboratory testing, including the LD-50 tests. Many people, of course, recoil at the thought of rats. Yet rats can be active, playful, and clean if given the appropriate environment, and many people report that they make affectionate and pleasing pets. One such satisfied human companion of a pet rat reported that his rat, named Weebee, would click his teeth, flick his tongue in and out, and open his eyes wide whenever he spoke to him. His human friend named this behavior "Weebee-pop-out-talk-with-eye-pops" and when Weebee was sitting in his hand, he would utter that phrase and Weebee would oblige him. Rats are not the only animals used for testing, however; rabbits, dogs (usually beagles), cats, and monkeys also are used.

Eve completed her kitchen cleanup; the custard now safely out of the oven. She thought she would pay a few bills, and then do a bit of autumn gardening — some more mulching, clipping, and pruning would help her beloved plants successfully survive whatever the winter had in store. But first the bills. Eve looked at the small stack of bills on the desk, relieved that it wasn't higher; she wanted to get outside before the warmth of the waning autumn sun faded. She remembered when she and Rob were just starting out how she had dreaded bill-paying time, always having to juggle who got paid when. They weren't rich now, but they were comfortable. Both Eve and Rob felt grateful for their success, and committed to "reinvesting" — their term for finding ways to express gratitude for their good fortune. They did this by tithing at their church, and contributing to selected charities. Having a tender feeling for dogs since she was a child, Eve always gave to the local humane society. They needed the contributions to care for the never-ending supply of abandoned dogs and cats that showed up at their doorstep. Eve had heard a shocking statistic the other day: Was it seven million dogs and cats euthanized every year? Her mind flickered to the idea of Pepper in a pound, but it was too painful to think of and she quickly turned away from the thought. With a shudder, she sealed the envelope. "Enough morbid thinking," Eve thought to herself. "Out to the garden and the sunshine!"

After sitting, it felt good to Eve to pull the bags of mulch over to the trees. She loved the feeling of the garden; it brought her back in touch with the life teeming around her, and restored the sense of a divine presence. The older Eve grew, the more important her spiritual life became. As she was spreading the mulch, Eve recalled something she had read that particularly appealed to her, and to which she invariably returned: Any activity, no matter how seemingly mundane, presents an opportunity for a spiritual experience. You don't have to be praying; you don't have to be doing something dramatic. You could be simply mulching your garden. "It's a line from a poem — Rilke," she recalled. "It goes something like 'If one paints or another plows — all is prayer.'" To her that perfectly summed up the nature of prayer. Eve completed her gardening and returned to the house to get ready for the family dinner.

The family enjoyed their evening together. David appreciated the meal; everyone licked their lips after the dessert in complete satisfaction. And the video was also a success. Full of good food and affection, the family sprawled around the living room to watch *Babe*. At one point Eve thought to herself, "We are just like a bunch of piglets in a litter." At times during the movie, a thought relating their pork dinner and the movie began to form in the back of Eve's mind. But it never quite emerged. "Stop the morbid thinking," she reminded herself again. "It's only a movie, so let yourself enjoy it."

After the family had gone, Eve and Rob cleaned the kitchen together, realigned the living room so that cushions and chairs were all at the correct angles again, and took out the trash. They took this time to recount the evening with one another, and to plan their activities for the next day. It would start with church, where Eve and Rob both served on a number of committees, and would definitely include a walk with Pepper along the park trail a half-hour ride away. Satisfied that their home was again in the right order, Eve and Ross climbed the stairs to go to bed.

Once again, a number of animals entered Eve's life as she cleaned the kitchen: The dish soap she used was tested on an animal, as was the plastic coating for the storage container where she placed leftovers. Twelve more animals were added to Eve's tally. By the end of the evening, Eve's animals numbered seventy-two.

As she did every evening, Eve read from a book of daily devotions comprising quotations from the Bible. She liked to think of the passage as she went to bed. Tonight she read from Proverbs 8:11, "For wisdom is better than rubies; and all the things that may be desired are not to be compared to it." "Good karma," she thought, mixing religious metaphors. Ready now, Eve turned out the light, and as she did every evening, turned toward her husband. Cupping her body around his, she felt the soothing familiarity of Rob against her. Eve usually slipped into sleep quite peacefully. But tonight, as she lay next to Rob, who was snoring softly in the dark, she felt a physical unease she couldn't quite identify. "Something I ate didn't sit well with me," she thought. "Maybe I have a guilty conscious over that extravagant dinner." Eve took some antacid tablets, hoping these would quiet her body enough to induce sleep. But whatever ailed her seemed like more than simple indigestion — she felt a general sense of unease.

Finally Eve fell into unsettled sleep. A few hours later she awakened, after a disturbingly vivid dream. She was sitting down to dinner with her family, as she actually had done earlier that evening. But now an additional person sat at the table, a man she couldn't identify at first, but who cast an ominous presence. Eve felt an undercurrent of dread and apprehension in the dream as she sat with this man. The outward reality of the scene did not match her feelings; everybody in the dream was conversing in a friendly and engaged manner. As the meal continued, Eve's terror grew until she awoke with her heart pounding and her palms sweating.

Even though she had escaped her dream, feelings of dread lingered as she lay in the dark. "Who was that man and why was he so creepy?" Eve wondered to herself. Much like a light switch flicking on to illuminate a darkened room, something clicked in her brain. She knew who he was. The frightening man in Eve's dream combined the features of the kindly farmer in *Babe* with another figure — but this one was quite sinister. The second likeness was an assassin who had been sent to kill a renegade God figure in another television show, *The X-Files*. "No wonder I was so frightened," Eve thought. "The guy was both kindly and fiendishly savage at the same time — someone sent to murder the good in us. Why did I ever think of that?" Eve didn't figure out her dream that night, but she resolved to talk to someone about it the next day. She was too exhausted from the emotional exertion to delve further into its meaning. Once again she lapsed into a troubled sleep.

God's Lure to Life: Emily the Cow

Eve's animals will sleep, too. Some of them may have dreams that comfort and soothe, although they will not come from their own personal memories. Perhaps there is a genetic memory, which will allow them to experience what it is like to live naturally, if only in their dreams. But they will never feel replenished from their slumber as Eve usually is, and they will never feel the calm reassurance of another being, as Eve does. They will lead a very different life from Eve's. Most of the humans they will encounter in their shortened and tortured lives will not see them as living beings.

These creatures, who, like us, are members of the animal kingdom, are also, like us, sentient beings. As sentient beings they can suffer, and in their suffering they experience pain similar to ours. We share so much with animals — the desire to live, to avoid pain, to be free to pursue our natural interests. There are, of course, important differences between human animals and other animals. Yet, as moral philosopher Tom Regan has pointed out, "Beneath the differences, there is sameness. Like us...animals embody the mystery and wonder of consciousness. Like us, they are not only in the world, they are aware of it. Like us, they are the psychological centers of a life that is uniquely their own."[11]

Animals cannot tell us in words that they suffer; but they tell us in many other ways that are obvious to those who pay attention. They groan and scream, whimper and grunt. They flinch, tremble, and recoil. They bang their heads, chew on the bars of their cages and on one another. They develop illnesses and many times their bodies refuse to work. Yet still they struggle to survive. Like us, they want to live, and they want to avoid pain and suffering.

There is a biological explanation for an animal's survival instinct: the will to live promotes the adaptive continuation of the species. But where does this will to be originate? We all seem to have it, both human and nonhuman animals.

Some say this will to live comes from God. In describing the agency of God in creation, theologian Jay McDaniel talks about how God "lures" us into life. "This lure is God immanent in us as an agent of our well-being, as Holy Spirit," he writes, adding that it is present in nonhuman life as well. "The lure of God's Spirit is that by which nonhuman organisms are inspired to live from moment to moment...."[12]

Emily the cow, now quite famous in some circles, is living testimony to a nonhuman animal's capacity to feel God's enticement to life. As reported by Kirsten Rosenberg in the magazine *Animals' Agenda*, "For many, the story of Emily's fight for life has been a spiritual awakening."[13] Emily's story began as she was headed for a slaughterhouse in Hopkinton, Massachusetts. Like many cows going to slaughter, Emily sensed what lay ahead. Deciding to act rather than to submit, however, Emily propelled her entire 1,400 pounds over a five-foot-high fence and escaped into the surrounding woods. Rosenberg describes Emily's ordeal: "Reminiscent of a Biblical odyssey, for 40 days and 40 nights this courageous cow eluded her captors, enduring severe snowstorms and freezing temperatures, all the while foraging for sustenance." The media picked up on Emily's plight and local human sympathizers began leaving stashes of hay for her. Then a couple who had been closely following Emily's saga, Meg and Lewis Randa, convinced the slaughterhouse owner to sell Emily to them for $1.

After many days the Randas finally coaxed a frightened Emily, who was by now very wary of humans, into their sanctuary at Peace Abbey. Today Emily lives contentedly, her trust in humans restored. Her fight for life inspired all of those who heard about it, and she has become something of a celebrity. Hundreds of well-wishers visit Peace Abbey to meet her, inspired by her courage and determination to live, and touched by her willingness to trust again. After becoming acquainted with Emily, some people swear off red meat or become full vegetarians. One couple was so taken with her that Emily became a bridesmaid at their wedding![14]

Why did Emily bolt out of the truck? Perhaps she felt God's lure especially strongly, and some inner well of strength enabled her to respond. All living beings, whether they can act or not, feel this lure. Too often it is human beings who contradict and interfere with God's appeal to life, denying the animal God's invitation.

The sheer scale and senselessness of animals' suffering is hard to absorb. No matter how much it seems that such suffering couldn't be possible, the sad fact is that it is only too real. Animal suffering in this country occurs every day, week, month, and year. When we encounter these devastating accounts, we invariably question them. Disbelief is the first defense against such monumental suffering. Beyond disbelief, however, is the opportunity to open ourselves with full awareness to the sacredness of all of creation. Disbelief casts a shadow, obscuring a potential spiritual path; awareness helps light the way.

The Message of Eve's Dream: The World As God's Body

Eve understood that awareness and compassion compose the vital and basic foundation through which our psychological and spiritual healths are joined. Every day she reflected on her existence with the intent of leading a good life. Yet, as we have seen, Eve was not aware that her daily decisions affected the lives of so many animals. She was, however, beginning to experience a spiritual disequilibrium, which would give her the opportunity to expand her awareness, and thus achieve further spiritual growth. The specific cause of her imbalance was not rising to the conscious level; but her dream brought it to her attention as only dreams can.

Eve's life, like all of our lives, is intimately connected to animals. She deeply loves Pepper; she also enjoys her encounters with squirrels, occasional deer, and the various birds that surround her feeder and peck the berries from the trees in her yard. Many more of the animals linked to Eve's life — and to all of our lives — remain unseen and unheard: behind the doors of laboratories, or out of sight, living and dying in the wild. And although we occasionally see animals in zoos or circuses, we fail to really understand their lives in captivity, to realize how their life spans are shortened, how the stress of confinement and isolation creates untold neuroses. We also fail to see the animals trapped behind the walls and fences of factory farms. We do, however, encounter animals every day in the food we eat, albeit in very altered form. The fact of their existence is literally at our fingertips every day. It's not surprising that Eve's connection to the food she was eating first drew her awareness to her effect on animals.

Eve was suffering from spiritual indigestion. At an unconscious level, she was coming to understand that all sentient beings deserve life, and will fight to protect it. Her dream merging the evil murderer with the kindly farmer pointed to an emerging conflict: When was it okay to take an animal's life? Is that life being taken away from God? In harming a living creature are we also harming God? Some theologians believe that when any one of God's creatures suffers, so does God.[15] Although Eve could not express these questions in words, her dream's images were perhaps subconsciously acknowledging her partial role as the "good-killer."

Because she is a searcher, Eve will pursue the direction in which the dream led her. In so doing Eve very well could encounter the idea that to harm a living creature is to harm God and, conversely, to revere the life of any creature is to revere God.[16] She could come across the comparison that God is to the world as a mind is to its body. Building the analogy, some theologians explain that we are related to our bodies in two ways: as agents and as patients. As agents we act *in* and *through* our bodies. We are acting as agents, for example, when we desire something to eat; we search out food, and we eat it. The sensations associated with satisfying our desire we experience as ourselves. We generated the desire and the eating, and we experience the satisfaction. When we are patients, however, our experiences do not originate out of our own agency. We are on the receiving end in these cases, such as discovering that one has cancer.

Our relationship to our bodies as both agents and patients parallels God's relationship to the world, which is God's body. Like us with our bodies, God is both an agent in the world and a patient. Sometimes God is on the receiving end also, so that despite God's wishes — as when one has cancer — events occur inside God's body that are outside God's agency.

In this Christian example, when the pig suffocates on the way to slaughter, when he is overcome with fear, when he struggles for life even as he nears his death, God suffers. In perfect empathy, and with an acute capacity to know all creatures deeply, God suffers alongside and within the tormented pig. God can and does suffer with the world. Therefore, when we inflict pain and suffering on another living being, we all — God, and all of the creatures in the vast web of life — are affected by that suffering in some way. Eve intuitively realized this through her dream, and the realization horrified and sickened her. And it will be her dis-ease with herself that will prompt her to reconsider her actions and to develop her awareness.

Spirituality and Mud-Bathing Elephants

For many of us, spiritual knowledge comes first from our intuitive feelings, rather than from our conscious minds. This capacity to intuit before we can articulate does not necessarily require a mystical explanation. In a research experiment using card games, psychologists discovered that the earlier people relied on their hunches to make judgments the better they did at the game. The psychologists explained that some earlier emotional memory, outside of the card players' conscious awareness, guided their judgment. Intuition, or hunches, do not appear out of the blue, but from an emotional experience from our past that resonates with our current situation.[17] Intuitive knowledge bubbles up from our dreams, appearing in the random thoughts that flicker through our minds, and in our *felt* senses of things.

All of us experience this, probably every day. I had intuitive reactions for years about my connection to the animals around me, but I dismissed them, filing them away in the back of my mind. On the few occasions I visited the circus, for example, or saw it on television, I felt repelled by the spectacle of beautiful wild creatures being forced to perform ridiculous tricks — tigers jumping through hoops of fire, a line of elephants, each with their forelegs on the backs of the elephant in front of them, forming an elephant conga line. For what real purpose were we bending the nature of these animals?

I have a photograph on my desk of five South African elephants, four adults and one youngster, in various poses of relaxed enjoyment in a large, muddy puddle of water. Their body language is clear: They are relishing the mud's cool relief from the hot, dry African summer. One female elephant, in particular, sits facing forward, hind legs relaxed outward, head back, her trunk raised in sheer, exuberant delight. Every time I look, or even think, of these elephants I smile with pleasure and am filled with their delight. The image of these magnificent living beings, expressing their true nature, resonates with authenticity.

Delighting in the elephants for what they are — not for what we can make them into — is integral to a spiritual relationship with animals. This delight can transform the space between us, which we have created because of our difference, from a potential barrier to a sacred place in which we encounter "animal presence."[18] When Buber said that it is "through our response to the creaturely Other [that] the unification of the world is achieved," he taught us that it is in "animal presence" that we may find a spiritual completeness.[19]

When we look at a circus elephant performing unnatural acts, we feel separate from her. She is the other that we observe, and are perhaps amused by; we identify the qualities that make her different from ourselves. When we can join with the other, something else happens. That something else is spiritual. When I look at my elated mud-bathing elephants, I am with them, right there, in their delight, filled with the joy of life *they are* in that moment. This feeling only lasts briefly, of course, as long as a spark of light. It is not, however, *just* a spark of light. The sparks from this and other moments illuminate a spiritual path that can guide us into a deeper relationship with all of creation.

It doesn't matter whether we orient ourselves toward a relationship with God, or with nature, or with the paradoxical Buddhist concept of the fullness found in emptiness. We can grasp the continuity of existence through our contact with another human being, or an elephant, our companion animal, a deer we encounter in a state park, or a dolphin. Species is not important; what is important is that the other is a being who appreciates life, is a part of life, and strives for life.

The invitation to discover a spiritual relationship with animals is, as Denise Levertov writes, to "Come into Animal Presence."[20] We come into animal presence when we share the joy of the mud-bathing elephants, thus accepting them for who they are, and entering their world, on their terms. And when we do, we find that

> *Those who were sacred have remained so,*
> *holiness does not dissolve, it is a presence*
> *of bronze, only the sight that saw it*
> *faltered and turned from it.*
> *An old joy returns in holy presence.*

A spiritual relationship with animals can return us to that "old joy in holy presence."

Epilogue

Animal grace has touched my life. The gift given me by the animals of this "great and mysterious and mute nation" saved me from spiritual despair.[1] They encouraged me to resume my search, that I might realize, and in that realization live, the unity of all existence. I have witnessed animals' ability to enjoy life in the face of profound physical decline; they seem able to accept "what is" much better than I. I have wondered at their unaffected beauty and grace as they fly, leap, trot, lope, dive, and slither. The willingness of so many animals to trust humans, even after being harmed, remains a marvel and a mystery. And to grasp that these "others" who seem so different in fact share so much with us moves me beyond measure.

Koko the gorilla grieved for her dead kitten and pondered the meaning of death in a sign-language interview; elephants, who also mourn their dead, have used their bodies to prop up ailing members of their herd; female rats have braved electrical shock as they crossed a researcher's grid to reach pups who were not their own; in another experiment monkeys refused to administer electric shock to other monkeys, even though they themselves were shocked as a result; a goose refused to leave the side of her mate who had been shot in the head with an arrow (he recovered and the pair were reunited). Lastly, an image of two chimps sitting side by side, their arms draped gently over one another's shoulders, gazing out at a red sunset, stays with me, a reminder of how much more alike we are than we may think.

The more we learn about the intelligence and emotional lives of nonhuman animals, the more we realize that differences between us and other species are more continuous than categorical; we are different by degree, not kind. We can no longer safely assume that human animals possess certain capacities — reasoning, grieving, altruism, a sense of a future — that nonhuman animals lack. The experiences of other animals are not so different from our own — they "play and grieve...have memories and a sense of the future for which they sometimes plan...they have a sense of home, of finding, seeking, returning to home. We know that when they face death, they fear it."[2] As we appreciate the richness of their lives, much of their "otherness" fades.

As animal grace helps me transcend the arbitrary boundary of species, it also helps me overcome other distinctions, such as race, gender, nationality, and religion — differences often used to exclude and exploit. I realize that these distinctions are more illusory than real, more superficial than enduring. For weaving itself throughout all our perceived differences is the pulse of life. All creatures who enjoy life seek fulfillment in whatever ways are suitable for them. That inherent impulse binds us to one another in the grand, creative web of existence. If one is speaking in religious terms, then that pulse of life comes from, or perhaps more accurately is, God. If God resides in any of us, then God resides in all of us — human and nonhuman animals alike.

I couldn't agree more with Susan Chernak McElroy, who said, "For all the grace that animals bring to us, I believe we are obliged to somehow gift them in return."[3] I feel that obligation; through my sense of accountability to them, I have found the means to resume my spiritual journey. The debt I feel toward animals is not a burden but rather another form of the gift they have given me. Just as the armature supports the sculpture, a sense of ethics supports my spirituality. Without such an internal structure, I believe my spirituality would be formless, folding into itself. I agree wholeheartedly with Stephanie Kaza, who said that spirituality is not merely about personal salvation but about moral responsibility and obligation as an interdependent part of being in the web of life.[4] If the great lesson is that we are all interconnected and, in fact, that we are all one, how could salvation — or enlightenment — end with the individual? I don't believe it could.

As much as I am capable of learning, animals have taught me about "attentive love." Attentive love, as ecofeminist Linda Vance explains, "requires more than simply asking, waiting, and hearing: it has to imply a commitment to action, and in particular, to action that will help preserve the other and let her flourish."[5]

Animal grace has made me more certain and more committed. Because of it, I can continue on my spiritual journey with renewed vigor. But now I do so with the realization that "enlightenment," or what Georg Feuerstein calls "lucid waking," does not just happen to us. "It calls for a deliberate act of will," he writes, "a *metanoia*, by which we consciously relate to life in a new way."[6]

One of the most significant ways I have chosen to relate to life in a new way was to join Isaac Bashevis Singer, who said, "Vegetarianism is my religion." I have amended that slightly to affirm, "Veganism is my religion." By that I mean that being a vegan is a daily spiritual practice in which I can honor the divine by respecting life and acknowledging the unity of existence. To me, being a vegan is the essence of ahimsa — the principle of conducting one's life so as to do no harm. As I noted in the chapter on ahimsa, it is a concept with reverberating significance. It requires maintaining an active and aware stance about one's conduct, as well as one's inner thoughts and feelings. It is not as much about *not* doing something as it is about bringing awareness of life's sanctity to everything we do. The Native American aphorism to "walk gently on the earth" captures this intent.

Gandhi said that ahimsa is the essential spiritual principle and that all others stem from it. The ideal of ahimsa guides me in choosing a spiritual practice, and in selecting from religious philosophies to inform me. I practice yoga daily, disciplining my body and breath and quieting my mind so that I might be receptive to the divine. As I continued my spiritual exploration, I gravitated toward those systems of thought that emphasize the unity of existence and that maintain that Spirit resides in all living creatures, not just in humans. In studying at the Vedanta Center of Greater Washington, D.C., I have come to appreciate Vedanta's view that no view of the infinite can be complete. All are necessarily partial — "the total truth resid[es] not in any one theory but in a synthesis in which all theories have their part."[7] I also found that spirit of tolerance and inclusiveness at the Unitarian Universalist Church, which draws upon a variety of religious traditions for its inspiration.

Although I still struggle with the concept of God, I find I cannot give it up. I do not think of God as an "entity" who can intervene in human life and I do not think of God as omnipotent. At times, however, I can grasp a sense of God as an abiding presence, or an ocean of consciousness that permeates and encompasses all existence. To me, the most useful metaphor for God is the one offered by Jay McDaniel, who says that God is to the world as a mind is to its body, which I described in chapter 7. A similarly appealing analogy is offered by Ramanuja, one of the great interpreters of Vedanta, who proposed that Braham — the all-pervading and divine being — is related to the cosmos as the soul is related to the body.

My spiritual understanding, however, is by no means complete. The question of innocent suffering still perplexes me. What can we make of the fact that countless nonhuman, and human, animals only experience pain and agony in their lives? For example, what relief, if any, does a veal calf ever experience? A few days after his birth, he will be cruelly removed from his mother and placed in a crate where he will be chained by the neck, unable to stand or to move, except for a few inches, in any direction. He will be deprived of any contact with other living beings. Kept in the dark except when fed, he will never see daylight or experience touch.

It is not just the veal calf who experiences such unremitting suffering, but all animals confined to circuses, factory farms, and research laboratories. Is this all there is for these millions of animals — suffering, more suffering, and then death? How can we understand that? Or more importantly, if we make an empathic connection with them in their tortured world, how can we *bear* it?

Human animals, of course, suffer too, and their anguish must also be recognized and alleviated. But I am concerned here about nonhuman animals, mainly because their suffering usually goes unrecognized and is tacitly supported by normative culture, the government, and other public and private institutions. "Animal abuse, like slavery in a slave society," Roberta Kalechofsky asserts, "is a fundamental underpinning of evil throughout society, paid for and voted for. Like the struggle against slavery, Animal Rights is part of the great attack upon the oldest of class presumptions — that there may be master and slaves and trafficking in living flesh."[8] Animals, then, are not only innocent sufferers; their suffering results from public and private policy, and is integral to the economic benefit of many of the powerful in human society.

Suffering — what causes it and how to transcend it — is at the heart of the Asian philosophies. We suffer because we are attached to our own desires and needs and because we falsely identify with our own egos rather than with our true nature, or the *real* self. As far as I can fathom, these traditions do not address the question of innocent suffering.

The German theologian Dorothee Soelle, in her book *Suffering*, proposes that the one thing everyone can do is bear active witness to the suffering. She asks the question, "Does...suffering serve God or the devil, the cause of becoming alive or being morally paralyzed?"[9] Gary Kowalski also emphasizes the importance of bearing active witness to suffering, for only then can suffering serve God.[10] We may not be able to intervene in the suffering of a particular victim, or alleviate it. But we can, and should become aware, and, with that awareness, take compassionate action. Both Kowalski and Soelle urge us to use suffering as a means to transform both our own lives and, slowly, the society we live in. Suffering must never be denied or forgotten. Although not specifically about suffering, Michael Fox's contention that spirituality is not valid unless it is also political essentially captures the same idea.[11]

In addition to actively witnessing another's anguish, solace can also be found in the idea that God is present to all who are tormented, especially if the sufferer can sense God's presence. But while I agree with the necessity of bearing witness and take comfort in the idea that God stands alongside the victim, I still long for something more — some hope that these pitiful beings will eventually find some relief. Jay McDaniel offers the hope — but not the certainty — that some kind of redemption provides transformation into a new state of existence. Instead of the veal calf's life consisting solely of pain and anguish, the calf may experience a fulfillment after death "appropriate to [his] own interests and needs." As I understand it, McDaniel suggests that only those who die unfulfilled would continue in this way. He emphasizes that "the hope is for a continuation of a sentient being's journey until completeness...is realized, after which death can be welcomed."[12] This explanation, then, does not offer the usual possibility of an afterlife for all who die. Only those who die with a sense of incompleteness — the inability to find fulfillment in life appropriate to their needs and interests — would be subject to this kind of redemption, because those who die complete would not need it. Speaking in Christian terms, McDaniel refers to "completeness" and "wholeness," while a Buddhist might refer to "enlightenment." While these are not exact equivalents, they are similar in that they point to achieving an ultimate state of existence. I cling to this proposal, knowing it is tenuous, to help me tolerate the knowledge that so many animals endure so much unremitting agony.

Related to the conundrum of innocent suffering is the question of who, or what, can suffer. One end of the spectrum, which might be called "radical relativism," doesn't differentiate between life forms. At first glance, this perspective seems to stem from a position of pure nondualism. In theory, equal value is assigned to all forms of existence, recognizing and protecting the continuity of existence. Put into practice on the relative plane of everyday existence, however, this moral relativism teeters on the brink of amorality. For example, proponents of "radical relativism" would consider a cow and a carrot to be of equal value, as well as morally equivalent. The degree of relativity becomes so extreme that the distinctions one needs in order to make ethical decisions are lost, or ignored. Simply stated, this view would argue that we don't know if grass suffers when you cut it, or if carrots experience pain, and therefore it is an unavoidable truth that it takes life to continue life, and pain often is necessary for the continuation of life. According to this logic, then, it is ethically acceptable to eat animals since we have to kill to live.

Most animals, and certainly all mammals, experience pain. The limbic system, a part of the brain that all mammals possess, is associated with the capacity to experience emotions — including desires — and the hypothalamus, a structure shared by all vertebrates, is involved in the ability to experience positive and negative emotions. Vegetables do not possess these neurological structures. So nonhuman animals, like human animals, are sentient — they feel pain and pleasure. Their lives include more complexity and texture than those of nonanimal life forms. Animals pursue interests, participate in social relationships, and form attachments. They plan, and clearly demonstrate, their preferences. But you don't have to refer to the scientific literature to support the judgment that cows experience pain. We know that they recoil, cry, groan, and writhe. A carrot does not.

One draws the inevitable conclusion that a significant difference exists between cows and carrots. And, I suspect, saying "please," "may I," and "thank you" before we kill an animal for its meat, as some relativists would propose, will do little to make up for their deaths.

I conclude this epilogue, but not my philosophical and spiritual inquiry. I feel increasingly that I have a philosophy and a practice that will nurture my spiritual development. I feel less certain about the future of our planet and its inhabitants. I would like to feel the optimism that Georg Feuerstein expresses with his conviction that "if one person can wake up, we all can!" and his faith "in the great potential and future of the human species."[13] Counterpoised to that attitude is the reflection made by Milan Kundera in his book *The Unbearable Lightness of Being:* "Humanity's true moral test, its fundamental test, consists of its attitude towards those who are at its mercy: animals. And in this respect, humankind has suffered a fundamental debacle, a debacle so fundamental that all others stem from it."

My competing levels of optimism or pessimism vary greatly. Sometimes I am sanguine; other times I am discouraged and riddled with frustration. But mostly I am somewhere in between. Although I waver between faith and doubt, I trust that my spiritual practice will guide me toward a future in which hope ultimately prevails. Wherever I find myself, I am determined to witness the suffering of innocent beings, and to do whatever I can to end it. If there is reason to hope, as Jane Goodall proposes, it will require, she says, a concerted effort on the part of all of humanity. We must reach beyond "the prison of our own lives, seeking reunion with the Spiritual Power" if we hope to save the world and its inhabitants. "We will have to evolve, all of us," Goodall writes, "from ordinary, everyday human beings — into saints! Ordinary people, like you and me, will have to become saints, or at least mini-saints."[14]

As I have emphasized throughout *Animal Grace*, we can interweave a spiritual relationship with animals into our everyday lives without having to discard, or ignore, other concerns. Every time we base our choices about the food we eat, the clothes we wear, and the products we use upon the effects those decisions have on animals, we honor the unity of existence and also grow spiritually. The application of awareness and the practice of compassion transform these prosaic transactions into spiritual events, and offer us one way to work toward the goal of becoming, at least, "mini-saints."

Once again, I end where I began: with my gratitude for the gift of animal grace and my commitment to honor that gift and those who bestowed it upon me.

Notes

Introduction

1. Kenneth J. Shapiro, *Bodily Reflective Modes: A Phenomenological Method for Psychology* (Durham, North Carolina: Duke University Press, 1985).

2. Peter Singer, *Animal Liberation: A New Ethics for Our Treatment of Animals* (New York: A New York Review Book, 1975).

3. Mary Lou Randour, *Women's Psyche, Women's Spirit: The Reality of Relationships* (New York: Columbia University Press, 1987).

4. Jim Mason and Peter Singer, *Animal Factories* (New York: Harmony Books, 1990); Zoe Weil, *Animals in Society: Facts and Perspectives on Our Treatment of Animals* (Jenkintown, Pennsylvania: Animalearn, 1991).

5. Thich Nhat Hanh, "Foreword," in Joan Halifax, *A Buddhist Life in America* (New York: Paulist Press, 1998), p. 2.

6. Joanna Macy, *World as Lover, World as Self* (Berkeley, California: Parallax Press, 1991), p. 35.

7. Susan Chernak McElroy, *Animals as Guides for the Soul* (New York: Ballantine/Wellspring, 1998), p. 29.

8. Jay B. McDaniel, *Of God and Pelicans: A Theology of Reverence for Life* (Louisville, Kentucky: Westminster/John Knox Press, 1989), p. 13.

9. John Cobb, "Foreword," in McDaniel, *Of God and Pelicans*, p. 12.

10. Isaac Bashevis Singer, "Foreword," in Dudley Giehl, *Vegetarianism: A Way of Life* (New York: Harper & Row, 1979).

11. Roshi Philip Kapleau, *To Cherish All Life: A Buddhist View of Animal Slaughter and Meat Eating* (Rochester, New York: The Zen Center, 1981), p. 19 and back page.

12. Josephine Donovan and Carol J. Adams, eds., *Beyond Animal Rights: A Feminist Caring Ethic for the Treatment of Animals*, (New York: Continuum, 1996); Gary Kowalski, *The Souls of Animals*, 2nd ed. (Walpole, New Hampshire: Stillpoint Publishing, 1999); Susan Chernak McElroy, *Animals as Teachers and Healers* (New York: Ballantine, 1996); Michael Fox, *Eating with Conscience: The Bioethics of Food* (Troutdale, Oregon: New Sage Press, 1997); Mason and Singer, *Animal Factories*; Jeffrey Moussaieff Masson and Susan McCarthy, *When Elephants Weep: The Emotional Lives of Animals* (New York: Dell Publishing, 1995); Evelyn Pluhar, *Beyond Prejudice: The Moral Significance of Human and Nonhuman Animals* (Durham, North Carolina: Duke U. Press, 1995); Tom Regan, *The Case for Animal Rights* (Berkeley: U. of California Press, 1983); John Robbins, *Diet for a New America* (Walpole, New Hampshire: Stillpoint Publishing, 1987); Richard D. Ryder, *Victims of Science: The Use of Animals in Research* (London: Davis-Poynter, 1975); Singer, *Animal Liberation*.

13. I am indebted to Rev. Al Kershaw, Episcopal priest, who made this idea central to all of his sermons and which guided the way he led his life. It is an idea that rings like a bell in my mind, calling me to life.

Chapter One

1. Nicholas J. Saunders, *Animal Spirits* (New York: Little, Brown and Company, 1995).

2. Stephen H. Webb, *On God and Dogs: A Christian Theology of Compassion for Animals* (New York: Oxford University Press, 1998).

3. Ibid., p. 103.

4. Lois Crisler, "Living with a Wolf Pack," in *Sisters of the Earth*, Lorraine Anderson, ed. (New York: Vintage Books, 1991), p. 215.

5. Jim Nollman, "The Secret Language of the Wild," *Utne Reader* (April, 1998): p. 40–45, 100.

6. Stephen Levine, "The Moment of Death: A View from the Other Side," *Utne Reader* (April, 1998): p. 77.

7. Susan Chernak McElroy, *Animals as Teachers and Healers: True Stories and Reflections* (New York: Ballantine Books, 1996), pp. 15–18.

8. Jeffrey Masson, *Dogs Never Lie About Love* (New York: Crown Publishers, 1997), p. 41.

9. Bonnie Smith, "Pets and Their People — Emotional Ties and Physical Benefits," *Animal Guardian*, vol. 10, no. 4 (1997): 8–9.

10. Karen Allen and J. L. Izzo, Jr., "Social Support and Resting Blood Pressure Among Young and Elderly Women: The Moderating Role of Pet Dogs and Cats," *Psychosomatic Medicine* 59 (1997): p. 94.

11. Karen Allen, Jim Blascovich, Joe Tomaka, Robert Kelsey, "Presence of Human Friends and Pet Dogs as Moderators of Autonomic Responses to Stress in Women," *Journal of Personality and Social Psychology* vol. 61, no. 4 (1991): pp. 582–589.

12. Karen Allen, "Anger and Hostility among Married Couples: Pet Dogs as Moderators of Cardiovascular Reactivity to Stress," *Psychosomatic Medicine* vol. 58 (1996): pp. 59–70.

13. Karen Allen, "Social Interaction and Cardiovascular Reactivity within Marriage: A Focus on Couples with and without Pet Cats and Dogs," *Psychosomatic Medicine* vol. 60 (1998): p. 100.

14. Paul Walsh and Peter Martin, "The Training of Pets as Therapy Dogs in a Women's Prison: A Pilot Study," *Anthrozoos* 7 (1994): pp. 124–128.

15. James Moneymaker and James Strimple, "Animals and Inmates: A Sharing Companionship behind Bars," *Journal of Offender Rehabilitation* 16 (1991): pp. 133–152.

16. Katharine Fick, "The Influence of an Animal on Social Interactions of Nursing Home Residents in a Group Setting," *American Journal of Occupational Therapy* 47 (1993): pp. 529–534; Judith Gammonley and Judy Yates, "Pet Projects: Animal-Assisted Therapy in Nursing Homes," *Journal of Gerontological Nursing* 17 (1991): pp. 12–15; Joel S. Savishinsky, "Intimacy, Domesticity and Pet Therapy with the Elderly: Expectation and Experience Among Nursing Home Volunteers," *Social Science and Medicine* 34 (1992): pp. 1325–1334; Rosemary G. Hoffman, "Companion Animals: A Therapeutic Measure for Elderly Patients," *Journal of Gerontological Social Work* 18 (1991): pp. 195–205; Tracy L. Chinner and Frank R. Dalziel, "An Exploratory Study of the Viability and Efficacy of a Pet-Facilitated Therapy Project within a Hospice," *Journal of Palliative Care* 7 (1991): pp. 13–20.

17. Roger Fouts with Stephen Tukel Mills, *Next of Kin: What Chimpanzees Have Taught Me about Who We Are* (New York: William Morrow and Company, Inc., 1997).

18. Masson, *Dog Never Lie About Love*, p. 49.

19. Gene Myers, *Children and Animals: Social Development and Our Connection to Other Species* (Boulder,

Colorado: Westview Press, 1998), p. 17.

20. Paul Shepard, *Thinking Animals: Animals and the Development of Human Intelligence* (New York: Viking Press, 1978).

21. Webb, *On God and Dogs*, p. 45.

22. Jon Wynne-Tyson, "Odd Boy In," *Between the Species* (April, 1998), p. 56.

23. Myers, *Children and Animals.*

24. Webb, *On God and Dogs*, p. 89.

25. Martin Buber, *The Way of Response. Selections of His Writings*, N. N. Glatzer, ed. (New York: Schocken Books, 1996), p. 136.

26. Jane Goodall, *Through a Window: My Thirty Years with the Chimpanzees of Gombe* (Boston: Houghton-Miflin, 1990).

27. Fouts, *Next of Kin.*

28. Jeffrey Moussaieff Masson and Susan McCarthy, *When Elephants Weep: The Emotional Lives of Animals* (New York: Dell Publishing, 1995).

Chapter Two

1. Mary Lou Randour, *Women's Psyche, Women's Spirit* (New York: Columbia U. Press, 1987), p. 125.

2. Stephen Mitchell, *Relational Concepts in Psychoanalysis* (Cambridge: Harvard University Press, 1988); Daniel N. Stern, *The Interpersonal World of the Infant* (New York: Basic Books, Inc., 1985).

3. Francis H. Cook, *Hua-yen Buddhism: The Jewel Net of Indra* (University Park: The Pennsylvania State University Press, 1981), p. 2.

4. Peter Matthiessen, *Nine-Headed Dragon River* (Boston: Shambhala Press, 1987), p. 7.

5. Georg Feuerstein, *Lucid Waking; Mindfulness and the Spiritual Potential of Lucid Waking* (Rochester, Vermont: Inner Traditions International, 1997), p. xvi.

6. Jay McDaniel, *Of God and Pelicans: A Theology of Reverence for Life* (Louisville, Kentucky: Westminster/John Knox Press, 1989), p. 15.

7. D. T. Suzuki, *Outlines of Mahayana Buddhism* (New York: Schocken Books, 1963).

8. The Buddhist notions of karma and reincarnation are elegantly complex and too often are simplified beyond their original meaning. Obviously, it is not my intent to do so here.

9. Buddhist Alliance for Social Engagement. Buddhist Peace Fellowship, P.O. Box 4650, Berkeley, California 94704.

10. Joanna Macy, *World as Lover, World as Self* (Berkeley, California: Parallax Press, 1991).

11. Betsy Swart, "The Chimp Farm," *The Great Ape Project: Equality Beyond Humanity*, Paola Cavalieri, ed., Peter Singer, contributor (New York: St. Martin's Press, 1995), pp. 291–295.

12. Swami Prabhavananda, *The Spiritual Heritage of India* (Hollywood, California: Vedanta Press, 1963), pp. 235–236.

13. Mary Phillips, "Savages, Drunks, and Lab Animals: The Researcher's Perception of Pain," *Society and Animals*, vol. 1 (1993): pp. 66–67.

14. "Animals in Laboratories," The Humane Society of the United States. Washington, D.C.

15. Phillips, "Savages, Drunks, and Lab Animals."

16. Kenneth Joel Shapiro, *Animal Model of Human Psychology: Critique of Science, Ethics and Policy* (Seattle: Hogrefe and Huber, 1998).

17. Phillips, "Savages, Drunks, and Lab Animals," pp. 76–77.

18. Tom Regan, "The Bird in the Cage: A Glimpse of My Life," *Between the Species*, vol. 2 (1986): pp. 42–49 and 90–100.

19. Donald R. Griffin, *Animal Minds* (Chicago: U of Chicago Press, 1992); R. J. Hoage and Larry Goldman (eds.), Preface, *Animal Intelligence: Insights into the Animal Mind* (Washington, D.C.: Smithsonian Institution Press, 1986); William Hodos, "The Evolution of the Brain and the Nature of Animal Intelligence," *Animal Intelligence*; Evelyn B. Pluhar, *Beyond Prejudice: The Moral Significance of Human and Nonhuman Animals* (Durham: Duke U. Press, 1996); Carolyn Ristau, "Do Animals Think?" *Animal Intelligence*.

20. Griffin, *Animal Minds*, pp. 3–4.

21. Carol Adams, "Caring about Suffering: A Feminist Exploration," *Beyond Animal Rights: A Feminist Ethic for the Treatment of Animals*, Josephine Donovan and Carol J. Adams, eds. (New York: Continuum, 1996), p. 193.

22. Peter Singer, *Animal Liberation: A New Ethics for Our Treatment of Animals* (New York: A New York Review Book, 1975), p. iv.

23. Charles Hartshorne, *Omnipotence and Other Theological Mistakes* (Albany, New York: State University of New York, 1984).

24. Macy, *World as Lover, World as Self*.

25. Thomas Moore, *The Re-enchantment of Everyday Life* (New York: HarperCollins, 1996), p. x.

26. Michael W. Fox, "Autobiographical Notes," *Between the Species* 3 (1987): pp. 98–99.

27. Ibid., p. 132.

Chapter Three

1. Richard A. Young, *Is God a Vegetarian? Christianity, Vegetarianism, and Animal Rights* (Chicago: Open Court, 1999).

2. J. R. Hyland, *The Slaughter of Terrified Beasts: A Biblical Basis for the Humane Treatment of Animals* (Sarasota, Florida: Viatoris Ministries, 1988), p. 1.

3. Ibid., p. 2.

4. Ibid.

5. Georges H. Westbeau, *Little Tyke* (Wheaton Illinois: The Theosophical Publishing House, 1986).

6. Josephine Donovan and Carol J. Adams, eds., *Beyond Animal Rights: A Feminist Caring Ethic for the Treatment of Animals* (New York: Continuum, 1996).

7. Young, *Is God a Vegetarian?*, p. 21.

8. Ibid., p. 147.

9. Swami Prabhavananda, *The Spiritual Heritage of India* (Hollywood, California: The Vedanta Press, 1963).

10. J. R. Hyland, "Albert Schweitzer," *Humane Religion*, vol. 2, no. 5 (November/December 1997): p. 8.

Chapter Four

Roberta Kalechofsky and Rosa Rasiel, *The Jewish Vegetarian Cookbook* (Marblehead, Massachusetts: Micah Publications, 1997).

2. Michael Lerner, *Jewish Renewal: Path to Healing and Transformation* (New York: Grosset/Putnam, 1994); Arthur Waskow, "What is Eco-Kosher?" in *For a Future to Be Possible*, Thich Nhat Hanh

(Berkeley, California: Parallax Press, 1993).

3. Arthur Waskow, in *New Menorah*, Spring 1993, p. 1 as cited in Lerner, *Jewish Renewal*.

4. Arthur Waskow, *Down to Earth Judaism: Food, Money, Sex, and the Rest of Life* (New York: William Morrow, 1995), p. 135.

5. Lerner, *Jewish Renewal*, p. 340.

6. Personal communication, April 1999.

7. Kalechofsky and Rasiel, *The Jewish Vegetarian Cookbook*, p. 6.

8. Ibid.

9. Rabbi Yitzchak HaCohen Kook, "A Vision of Vegetarianism and Peace," in *Rabbis and Vegetarianism: An Evolving Tradition*, Roberta Kalechofsky, ed. (Marblehead, Massachusetts: Micah Publications, Inc., 1995), p. 6.

10. Rami M. Shapiro, *Minyan: Ten Principles for Living a Life of Integrity* (New York: Bell Tower, 1997), p. 149.

11. Kalechofsky and Rasiel, *The Jewish Vegetarian Cookbook*.

12. Richard A. Young, *Is God a Vegetarian? Christianity, Vegetarianism, and Animal Rights* (Chicago: Open Court, 1999).

13. Andrew Linzey, *Animal Theology* (Urbana, Illinois: University of Illinois Press, 1994).

14. Stephen H. Webb, *On God and Dogs: A Christian Theology of Compassion for Animals* (New York: Oxford University Press, 1998), p. 158.

15. Ibid.

16. Ibid., p. 166.

17. Steven Rosen, *Food for the Spirit: Vegetarianism and the World Religions* (New York: Bala Books, 1987), p. 77.

18. Roshi Philip Kapleau, *To Cherish All Life: A Buddhist View of Animal Slaughter and Meat Eating* (Rochester, New York: The Zen Center, 1981), p. 43.

19. Rabbi Michael L. Kramer, "A Personal Statement," in *Rabbis and Vegetarianism*, p. 45.

20. "Position of The American Dietetic Association: Vegetarian Diets." January 7, 1998. The American Dietetic Association, 216 West Jackson Boulevard, Chicago, Illinois 60606-6995.

21. Howard F. Lyman, with Glen Merzer, *Mad Cowboy: Plain Truth from the Cattle Rancher Who Won't Eat Meat* (New York: Scribner, 1998), p. 179.

22. Michael W. Fox, *Eating with Conscience: The Bioethics of Food* (Troutdale, Oregon: New Sage Press, 1997); Lyman, *Mad Cowboy*; John Robbins, *Diet for a New America* (Walpole, New Hampshire: Stillpoint Publishing, 1987).

Chapter Five

1. Christopher Key Chapple, *Nonviolence to Animals, Earth, and Self in Asian Traditions* (Albany, New York: State University of New York, 1993), p. 11.

2. Steven Rosen, *Food for the Spirit: Vegetarianism and the World Religions* (New York: Bala Books, 1987).

3. Wallace Slater, *Raja Yoga* (London: The Theosophical Publishing House, 1968).

4. Judith Lasater, "Beginning the Journey," *Yoga Journal* (December/January 1998): p. 42.

5. Eva Batt, "Why Veganism?" in *Here's Harmlessness: An Anthology of Ahimsa*, 5th ed. (Malaga, New Jersey: The American Vegan Society, 1993), p. 12.

6. Polly Young-Eisendrath and Martin Rafe, eds., *Awakening to Zen: The Teaching of Roshi Philip Kapleau* (New York: Scribner, 1997).

7. M. K. Gandhi, *Non-Violent Resistance* (New York: Schocken Books, 1951).

8. Georg Feuerstein, *Lucid Waking: Mindfulness and the Spiritual Potential of Humanity* (Rochester, Vermont: Inner Traditions International, 1997).

9. Walpola Rahula, *What the Buddha Taught* (New York: Grove Press, 1986).

10. Chapple, *Nonviolence to Animals, Earth, and Self in Asian Traditions*, p. xiv.

11. Ibid.

12. Lasater, "Beginning the Journey."

13. Feuerstein, *Lucid Waking*, p. 39.

14. Young-Eisendrath and Rafe, eds., *Awakening to Zen*, pp. 48–49.

15. Chapple, *Nonviolence to Animals, Earth, and Self in Asian Traditions*.

16. Clayborne Carson, ed., *The Papers of Martin Luther King, Jr., Volume III, Birth of a New Age: December 1955–December 1956* (Berkeley, California: University of California Press, 1997), p. 279.

17. Gandhi, *Non-Violent Resistance*.

18. Swami Prabhavananda and Christopher Isherwood, *How to Know God: The Yoga Aphorisms of Patanjali* (Hollywood, California: Vedanta Press, 1953).

19. Young-Eisendrath and Rafe, eds., *Awakening to Zen*.

20. Lora Grindlay, *The Province*, July 13, 1997.

21. Stephanie Kaza, "Field of Bright Spirit: Intimate Relations with the Natural World," *ReVision*, vol. 21, no. 2 (Fall 1998): p. 17.

22. Ibid., p. 19.

23. Carol J. Adams, *The Sexual Politics of Meat* (New York: Continuum, 1990), p. 40.

24. Personal communication, January 1999.

Chapter Six

1. Gary Kowalski, *The Souls of Animals*, 2nd ed. (Walpole, New Hampshire: Stillpoint, 1999), pp. 21–22.

2. Nicholas J. Saunders, *Animal Spirits* (New York: Little, Brown and Company, 1995).

3. Elizabeth Atwood Lawrence, "The Symbolic Role of Animals in the Plains Indians Sun Dance," *Society and Animals*, vol. 1, no. 1 (1993): pp. 17–37.

4. G. Naganathan, *Animal Welfare and Nature: Hindu Scriptural Perspectives* (Washington, D.C.: Center for Respect of Life and Environment, 1989), p. 2.

5. Thich Nhat Hanh, *Interbeing: Fourteen Guidelines for Engaged Buddhism*, 3rd ed. (Berkeley, California: Parallax Press, 1998).

6. Rynn Berry, *Food for the Gods: Vegetarianism and The World's Religions* (New York: Pythagorean Publishers, 1998), p. 104.

7. Steve Rosen, *Food for the Spirit: Vegetarianism and the World Religions* (New York: Bala Books, 1987), p. 98.

8. Swami Vivekananada, *The Complete Works of Swami Vivekananda*, Mayavati memorial edition, Volume II (Calcutta, India: Advaita Ashrama, 1987), p. 297.

9. Naganathan, *Animal Welfare and Nature*.

10. Polly Young-Eisendrath and Rafe Martin, eds., *Awakening to Zen: the Teachings of Roshi Philip Kapleau* (New York: Scribner, 1997).

11. Ibid., p. 43.

12. Richard Young, *Is God a Vegetarian? Christianity, Vegetarianism, and Animal Rights* (Chicago: Open Court, 1999).

13. J. R. Hyland, *The Slaughter of Terrified Beasts: A Biblical Basis for the Humane Treatment of Animals* (Sarasota, Florida: Viatoris Ministries, 1988).

14. Stephen H. Webb, *On God and Dogs: A Christian Theology of Compassion for Animals* (New York: Oxford University Press, 1998), p. 175.

15. Ibid.

16. Jay B. McDaniel, *Of God and Pelicans: A Theology of Reverence for Life* (Louisville, Kentucky: Westminster/John Knox Press, 1989).

17. *The Washington Post*, October 23, 1998, Section A1, pp. 8–9.

18. Michael W. Fox, *St. Francis of Assisi, Animals, and Nature.* (Washington, D.C.: Center for Respect for Life and Environment, 1989).

19. John Wesley, "The General Deliverance," in *Animals and Christianity,* Andrew Linzey and Tom Regan, eds. (New York: Crossroad, 1988), p. 102.

20. Rande Brown, "The Crown Exit: Phowa Teachings in Bodh Gaya," *Tricycle: The Buddhist Review* (Fall, 1997): p. 40.

21. Scott S. Smith, *Pet Souls: Evidence that Animals Survive Death* (Thousand Oaks, California: Light Source Research, 1994).

22. Kowalski, *The Souls of Animals*, pp. 49–50.

23. Martin Buber, *The Legend of the Baal-Shem*, trans. Maurice Friedman (New York: Schocken Books, 1969), p. 32.

Chapter Seven

1. "Change of Life Drug Premarin: A Bitter Pill to Swallow," *Friends of Animals,* January 1996; Patricia Jane Lemley, "The Truth about Premarin," *Pawprints* (Summer 1995): pp. 19–20.

2. Richard D. Ryder, *Victims of Science: The Use of Animals in Research* (London: David-Poynter, 1975).

3. Greta Nilson and others, *Facts about Furs* (Washington, D.C.: Animal Welfare Institute, 1980); Betsy Swart, "The Fight against Fur," *The Animals' Agenda* (July/August 1996).

4. Greta Nilson and others, *Facts about Furs.*

5. Jim Mason, "All Heaven in a Rage," in *All Heaven in a Rage: Speaking for Those Who Can't,* Laura A. Moretti, ed. (Canoga Park, California: MBK Publishing /The Animals' Voice Magazine, 1994), pp. 21–38; Jim Mason and Peter Singer, *Animal Factories* (New York: Harmony Books, 1990); Laura A. Moretti, "The Day the Earth Stood Still," *The Animals' Voice Magazine* (April/May 1991): p. 80; Andrew Tyler, "Getting Away with Murder," *All Heaven in a Rage*, pp. 66–76; Dudley Giehl, *Vegetarianism: A Way of Life* (New York: Harper and Row, 1979).

6. Erik Marcus, *Vegan: The New Ethics of Eating* (Ithaca, New York: McBooks Press, 1998); Mason and Singer, *Animal Factories*; Peter Singer, *Animal Liberation: A New Ethics for Our Treatment of Animals* (New York: A New York Review Book, 1979); Sue Coe, *Dead Meat* (New York: Four Walls Eight Windows, 1995).

7. Helga Tacreiter, "What Cows Do," *Humane Innovations and Alternatives,* vol. 8 (1994): p. 669.

8. Ryder, *Victims of Science.*

9. "The Facts about Animal Experimentation," Physicians Committee for Responsible Medicine.

10. Neal D. Bernard, M.D., "New Cell Tests Outperform Animal Tests," *Animal Guardian*, vol. 10, no. 1 (1997): pp. 6–7.

11. Tom Regan, "The Burden of Complicity," in Coe, *Dead Meat*, pp. 1–2.

12. Jay B. McDaniel, *Of God and Pelicans: A Theology of Reverence for Life* (Louisville, Kentucky: Westminster/John Knox Press, 1989), p. 39.

13. Kirsten Rosenberg, "Happy Endings: Putting a Face on Meat," *Animals' Agenda* (September/October, 1996): p. 34.

14. Ibid.

15. Charles Hartshorne, *Omnipotence and Other Theological Mistakes* (Albany: State University of New York, 1984).

16. McDaniel, *Of God and Pelicans*.

17. Sandra Blakeslee, "In Work on Intuition, Gut Feelings Are Tracked to Source: The Brain," *New York Times*, Science, March 4, 1997, B11.

18. Denise Levertov, "Animal Presence," in *Oblique Prayers* (New York: New Directions Publishing Corporation, 1984).

19. Robert E. Wood, *Martin Buber's Ontology* (Evanston, Illinois: Northwestern Press, 1969), p. 20.

20. Levertov, "Animal Presence."

Epilogue

1. Joy Williams, "The Inhumanity of the Animal People," *Harper's* (August 1997): p. 60.

2. Ibid., p. 60,

3. Susan Chernak McElroy, *Animals as Guides for the Soul* (New York: Ballantine/Wellspring, 1998), p. 47.

4. Personal communication, April 1999.

5. Linda Vance, "Beyond *Just-So Stories:* Narrative, Animals, and Ethics," in *Animals and Women: Feminist Theoretical Explorations*, Carol J. Adams and Josephine Donovan, eds. (Durham, North Carolina: Duke University Press, 1995), p. 184.

6. Georg Feuerstein, *Lucid Waking: Mindfulness and the Spiritual Potential of Lucid Waking* (Rochester, Vermont: Inner Traditions International, 1997), p. xvi.

7. Swami Prabhavananda, *The Spiritual Heritage of India* (Hollywood, California: Vedanta Press, 1979), p. 12.

8. Roberta Kalechofsky, *Autobiography of a Revolutionary: Essays on Animal and Human Rights* (Marblehead, Massachusetts: Micah Publications, 1991), p. v.

9. Dorothee Soelle, *Suffering,* trans. Everett R. Kalin (Minneapolis, Minnesota: Fortress Press, 1984).

10. Personal communication, April 1999.

11. Personal communication, April 1999.

12. Jay B. McDaniel, *Of God and Pelicans: A Theology of Reverence for Life* (Louisville, Kentucky: Westminster/John Knox Press, 1989), p. 47.

13. Feuerstein, *Lucid Waking*, pp. xvii and xviii.

14. Jane Goodall, with Philip Berman, *Reason for Hope: A Spiritual Journey* (New York: Warner Books, 1999), p. 200.

Index

About the Author

Mary Lou Randour, Ph.D., a professional psychologist, is director of programs for Psychologists for the Ethical Treatment of Animals and a consultant to the Doris Day Animal Foundation. After sixteen years in private practice, she now devotes herself to the animal advocacy movement. She serves on several boards and committees and lobbies to pass legislation benefiting animals. She is the author of *Women's Psyche, Women's Spirit: The Reality of Relationships* and editor of *Exploring Sacred Landscapes: Religious and Spiritual Experiences in Psychotherapy*, both published by Columbia University Press. Mary Lou lives with her husband, Sam Black, and her two beloved canine companions, Toshi and Sophie, in Chevy Chase, Maryland.

New World Library is dedicated to publishing
books, cassettes, and videotapes that inspire and challenge us
to improve the quality of our lives and the world.

New World Library
14 Pamaron Way
Novato, CA 94949

Phone: (415) 884-2100
Fax: (415) 884-2199
Or call toll-free (800) 972-6657
Catalog Requests: Ext. 50
Ordering: Ext. 52

E-mail: escort@nwlib.com
http://www.nwlib.com